ISBN 0-8373-1195-0

C-1195 **CAREER EXAMINATION SERIES**

This is your
PASSBOOK® for...

Cleaner/ Maintainer's Helper

Test Preparation Study Guide
Questions & Answers

NATIONAL LEARNING CORPORATION®

Copyright © 2019 by
National Learning Corporation

212 Michael Drive, Syosset, NY 11791
(516) 921-8888 • www.passbooks.com
E-mail: info@passbooks.com

PUBLISHED IN THE UNITED STATES OF AMERICA

3 1327 00669 9581

PASSBOOK® SERIES

THE *PASSBOOK® SERIES* has been created to prepare applicants and candidates for the ultimate academic battlefield – the examination room.

At some time in our lives, each and every one of us may be required to take an examination – for validation, matriculation, admission, qualification, registration, certification, or licensure.

Based on the assumption that every applicant or candidate has met the basic formal educational standards, has taken the required number of courses, and read the necessary texts, the *PASSBOOK® SERIES* furnishes the one special preparation which may assure passing with confidence, instead of failing with insecurity. Examination questions – together with answers – are furnished as the basic vehicle for study so that the mysteries of the examination and its compounding difficulties may be eliminated or diminished by a sure method.

This book is meant to help you pass your examination provided that you qualify and are serious in your objective.

The entire field is reviewed through the huge store of content information which is succinctly presented through a provocative and challenging approach – the question-and-answer method.

A climate of success is established by furnishing the correct answers at the end of each test.

You soon learn to recognize types of questions, forms of questions, and patterns of questioning. You may even begin to anticipate expected outcomes.

You perceive that many questions are repeated or adapted so that you can gain acute insights, which may enable you to score many sure points.

You learn how to confront new questions, or types of questions, and to attack them confidently and work out the correct answers.

You note objectives and emphases, and recognize pitfalls and dangers, so that you may make positive educational adjustments.

Moreover, you are kept fully informed in relation to new concepts, methods, practices, and directions in the field.

You discover that you are actually taking the examination all the time: you are preparing for the examination by "taking" an examination, not by reading extraneous and/or supererogatory textbooks.

In short, this PASSBOOK®, used directedly, should be an important factor in helping you to pass your test.

CLEANER/MAINTAINER'S HELPER

DUTIES

Cleaner/Maintainer's Helpers clean, sweep and wash buses, depots, garages, shops and other facilities as assigned. Assist maintainers in the servicing, maintenance, inspection and repair of buses and other automotive equipment. Perform other related duties as required.

Maintainer's Helpers assist in the maintenance, installation, inspection, testing, alteration and repair of bus and other electro-mechanical equipment; clean and lubricate bus parts; move bus parts and equipment using forklifts, hi-los, hoists, hand trucks and conveyors; measure tire pressure and change flat tires; check and maintain fluid levels of engine oil, batteries, radiators and windshield washer reservoirs; fuel buses; drain waste oil; sandblast parts; drive/shift buses and trucks; and perform related work.

SCOPE OF THE EXAMINATION

The multiple-choice test may include questions on the proper selection and use of tools and equipment used in the maintenance and repair of mechanical and electromechanical equipment; reading and interpreting written material; reading meters; taking measurements; and performing basic shop computations; understanding basic mechanical and electrical theory; knowledge of safe work practices and procedures; and other related areas.

HOW TO TAKE A TEST

I. YOU MUST PASS AN EXAMINATION

A. WHAT EVERY CANDIDATE SHOULD KNOW

Examination applicants often ask us for help in preparing for the written test. What can I study in advance? What kinds of questions will be asked? How will the test be given? How will the papers be graded?

As an applicant for a civil service examination, you may be wondering about some of these things. Our purpose here is to suggest effective methods of advance study and to describe civil service examinations.

Your chances for success on this examination can be increased if you know how to prepare. Those "pre-examination jitters" can be reduced if you know what to expect. You can even experience an adventure in good citizenship if you know why civil service exams are given.

B. WHY ARE CIVIL SERVICE EXAMINATIONS GIVEN?

Civil service examinations are important to you in two ways. As a citizen, you want public jobs filled by employees who know how to do their work. As a job seeker, you want a fair chance to compete for that job on an equal footing with other candidates. The best-known means of accomplishing this two-fold goal is the competitive examination.

Exams are widely publicized throughout the nation. They may be administered for jobs in federal, state, city, municipal, town or village governments or agencies.

Any citizen may apply, with some limitations, such as the age or residence of applicants. Your experience and education may be reviewed to see whether you meet the requirements for the particular examination. When these requirements exist, they are reasonable and applied consistently to all applicants. Thus, a competitive examination may cause you some uneasiness now, but it is your privilege and safeguard.

C. HOW ARE CIVIL SERVICE EXAMS DEVELOPED?

Examinations are carefully written by trained technicians who are specialists in the field known as "psychological measurement," in consultation with recognized authorities in the field of work that the test will cover. These experts recommend the subject matter areas or skills to be tested; only those knowledges or skills important to your success on the job are included. The most reliable books and source materials available are used as references. Together, the experts and technicians judge the difficulty level of the questions.

Test technicians know how to phrase questions so that the problem is clearly stated. Their ethics do not permit "trick" or "catch" questions. Questions may have been tried out on sample groups, or subjected to statistical analysis, to determine their usefulness.

Written tests are often used in combination with performance tests, ratings of training and experience, and oral interviews. All of these measures combine to form the best-known means of finding the right person for the right job.

II. HOW TO PASS THE WRITTEN TEST

A. *NATURE OF THE EXAMINATION*

To prepare intelligently for civil service examinations, you should know how they differ from school examinations you have taken. In school you were assigned certain definite pages to read or subjects to cover. The examination questions were quite detailed and usually emphasized memory. Civil service exams, on the other hand, try to discover your present ability to perform the duties of a position, plus your potentiality to learn these duties. In other words, a civil service exam attempts to predict how successful you will be. Questions cover such a broad area that they cannot be as minute and detailed as school exam questions.

In the public service similar kinds of work, or positions, are grouped together in one "class." This process is known as *position-classification*. All the positions in a class are paid according to the salary range for that class. One class title covers all of these positions, and they are all tested by the same examination.

B. *FOUR BASIC STEPS*

1) Study the announcement

How, then, can you know what subjects to study? Our best answer is: "Learn as much as possible about the class of positions for which you've applied." The exam will test the knowledge, skills and abilities needed to do the work.

Your most valuable source of information about the position you want is the official exam announcement. This announcement lists the training and experience qualifications. Check these standards and apply only if you come reasonably close to meeting them.

The brief description of the position in the examination announcement offers some clues to the subjects which will be tested. Think about the job itself. Review the duties in your mind. Can you perform them, or are there some in which you are rusty? Fill in the blank spots in your preparation.

Many jurisdictions preview the written test in the exam announcement by including a section called "Knowledge and Abilities Required," "Scope of the Examination," or some similar heading. Here you will find out specifically what fields will be tested.

2) Review your own background

Once you learn in general what the position is all about, and what you need to know to do the work, ask yourself which subjects you already know fairly well and which need improvement. You may wonder whether to concentrate on improving your strong areas or on building some background in your fields of weakness. When the announcement has specified "some knowledge" or "considerable knowledge," or has used adjectives like "beginning principles of…" or "advanced … methods," you can get a clue as to the number and difficulty of questions to be asked in any given field. More questions, and hence broader coverage, would be included for those subjects which are more important in the work. Now weigh your strengths and weaknesses against the job requirements and prepare accordingly.

3) Determine the level of the position

Another way to tell how intensively you should prepare is to understand the level of the job for which you are applying. Is it the entering level? In other words, is this the position in which beginners in a field of work are hired? Or is it an intermediate or advanced level? Sometimes this is indicated by such words as "Junior" or "Senior" in the class title. Other jurisdictions use Roman numerals to designate the level – Clerk I, Clerk II, for example. The word "Supervisor" sometimes appears in the title. If the level is not indicated by the title, check the description of duties. Will you be working under very close supervision, or will you have responsibility for independent decisions in this work?

4) Choose appropriate study materials

Now that you know the subjects to be examined and the relative amount of each subject to be covered, you can choose suitable study materials. For beginning level jobs, or even advanced ones, if you have a pronounced weakness in some aspect of your training, read a modern, standard textbook in that field. Be sure it is up to date and has general coverage. Such books are normally available at your library, and the librarian will be glad to help you locate one. For entry-level positions, questions of appropriate difficulty are chosen – neither highly advanced questions, nor those too simple. Such questions require careful thought but not advanced training.

If the position for which you are applying is technical or advanced, you will read more advanced, specialized material. If you are already familiar with the basic principles of your field, elementary textbooks would waste your time. Concentrate on advanced textbooks and technical periodicals. Think through the concepts and review difficult problems in your field.

These are all general sources. You can get more ideas on your own initiative, following these leads. For example, training manuals and publications of the government agency which employs workers in your field can be useful, particularly for technical and professional positions. A letter or visit to the government department involved may result in more specific study suggestions, and certainly will provide you with a more definite idea of the exact nature of the position you are seeking.

III. KINDS OF TESTS

Tests are used for purposes other than measuring knowledge and ability to perform specified duties. For some positions, it is equally important to test ability to make adjustments to new situations or to profit from training. In others, basic mental abilities not dependent on information are essential. Questions which test these things may not appear as pertinent to the duties of the position as those which test for knowledge and information. Yet they are often highly important parts of a fair examination. For very general questions, it is almost impossible to help you direct your study efforts. What we can do is to point out some of the more common of these general abilities needed in public service positions and describe some typical questions.

1) General information

Broad, general information has been found useful for predicting job success in some kinds of work. This is tested in a variety of ways, from vocabulary lists to questions about current events. Basic background in some field of work, such as sociology or economics, may be sampled in a group of questions. Often these are principles which have become familiar to most persons through exposure rather than through formal training. It is difficult to advise you how to study for these questions; being alert to the world around you is our best suggestion.

2) Verbal ability

An example of an ability needed in many positions is verbal or language ability. Verbal ability is, in brief, the ability to use and understand words. Vocabulary and grammar tests are typical measures of this ability. Reading comprehension or paragraph interpretation questions are common in many kinds of civil service tests. You are given a paragraph of written material and asked to find its central meaning.

3) Numerical ability

Number skills can be tested by the familiar arithmetic problem, by checking paired lists of numbers to see which are alike and which are different, or by interpreting charts and graphs. In the latter test, a graph may be printed in the test booklet which you are asked to use as the basis for answering questions.

4) Observation

A popular test for law-enforcement positions is the observation test. A picture is shown to you for several minutes, then taken away. Questions about the picture test your ability to observe both details and larger elements.

5) Following directions

In many positions in the public service, the employee must be able to carry out written instructions dependably and accurately. You may be given a chart with several columns, each column listing a variety of information. The questions require you to carry out directions involving the information given in the chart.

6) Skills and aptitudes

Performance tests effectively measure some manual skills and aptitudes. When the skill is one in which you are trained, such as typing or shorthand, you can practice. These tests are often very much like those given in business school or high school courses. For many of the other skills and aptitudes, however, no short-time preparation can be made. Skills and abilities natural to you or that you have developed throughout your lifetime are being tested.

Many of the general questions just described provide all the data needed to answer the questions and ask you to use your reasoning ability to find the answers. Your best preparation for these tests, as well as for tests of facts and ideas, is to be at your physical and mental best. You, no doubt, have your own methods of getting into an exam-taking mood and keeping "in shape." The next section lists some ideas on this subject.

IV. KINDS OF QUESTIONS

Only rarely is the "essay" question, which you answer in narrative form, used in civil service tests. Civil service tests are usually of the short-answer type. Full instructions for answering these questions will be given to you at the examination. But in case this is your first experience with short-answer questions and separate answer sheets, here is what you need to know:

1) Multiple-choice Questions

Most popular of the short-answer questions is the "multiple choice" or "best answer" question. It can be used, for example, to test for factual knowledge, ability to solve problems or judgment in meeting situations found at work.

A multiple-choice question is normally one of three types—

- It can begin with an incomplete statement followed by several possible endings. You are to find the one ending which *best* completes the statement, although some of the others may not be entirely wrong.
- It can also be a complete statement in the form of a question which is answered by choosing one of the statements listed.

- It can be in the form of a problem – again you select the best answer.

Here is an example of a multiple-choice question with a discussion which should give you some clues as to the method for choosing the right answer:

When an employee has a complaint about his assignment, the action which will *best* help him overcome his difficulty is to
A. discuss his difficulty with his coworkers
B. take the problem to the head of the organization
C. take the problem to the person who gave him the assignment
D. say nothing to anyone about his complaint

In answering this question, you should study each of the choices to find which is best. Consider choice "A" – Certainly an employee may discuss his complaint with fellow employees, but no change or improvement can result, and the complaint remains unresolved. Choice "B" is a poor choice since the head of the organization probably does not know what assignment you have been given, and taking your problem to him is known as "going over the head" of the supervisor. The supervisor, or person who made the assignment, is the person who can clarify it or correct any injustice. Choice "C" is, therefore, correct. To say nothing, as in choice "D," is unwise. Supervisors have and interest in knowing the problems employees are facing, and the employee is seeking a solution to his problem.

2) True/False Questions

The "true/false" or "right/wrong" form of question is sometimes used. Here a complete statement is given. Your job is to decide whether the statement is right or wrong.

SAMPLE: A roaming cell-phone call to a nearby city costs less than a non-roaming call to a distant city.

This statement is wrong, or false, since roaming calls are more expensive.

This is not a complete list of all possible question forms, although most of the others are variations of these common types. You will always get complete directions for answering questions. Be sure you understand *how* to mark your answers – ask questions until you do.

V. RECORDING YOUR ANSWERS

Computer terminals are used more and more today for many different kinds of exams.

For an examination with very few applicants, you may be told to record your answers in the test booklet itself. Separate answer sheets are much more common. If this separate answer sheet is to be scored by machine – and this is often the case – it is highly important that you mark your answers correctly in order to get credit.

An electronic scoring machine is often used in civil service offices because of the speed with which papers can be scored. Machine-scored answer sheets must be marked with a pencil, which will be given to you. This pencil has a high graphite content which responds to the electronic scoring machine. As a matter of fact, stray dots may register as answers, so do not let your pencil rest on the answer sheet while you are pondering the correct answer. Also, if your pencil lead breaks or is otherwise defective, ask for another.

Since the answer sheet will be dropped in a slot in the scoring machine, be careful not to bend the corners or get the paper crumpled.

The answer sheet normally has five vertical columns of numbers, with 30 numbers to a column. These numbers correspond to the question numbers in your test booklet. After each number, going across the page are four or five pairs of dotted lines. These short dotted lines have small letters or numbers above them. The first two pairs may also have a "T" or "F" above the letters. This indicates that the first two pairs only are to be used if the questions are of the true-false type. If the questions are multiple choice, disregard the "T" and "F" and pay attention only to the small letters or numbers.

Answer your questions in the manner of the sample that follows:

32. The largest city in the United States is
    A. Washington, D.C.
    B. New York City
    C. Chicago
    D. Detroit
    E. San Francisco

1) Choose the answer you think is best. (New York City is the largest, so "B" is correct.)
2) Find the row of dotted lines numbered the same as the question you are answering. (Find row number 32)
3) Find the pair of dotted lines corresponding to the answer. (Find the pair of lines under the mark "B.")
4) Make a solid black mark between the dotted lines.

VI. BEFORE THE TEST

Common sense will help you find procedures to follow to get ready for an examination. Too many of us, however, overlook these sensible measures. Indeed, nervousness and fatigue have been found to be the most serious reasons why applicants fail to do their best on civil service tests. Here is a list of reminders:

- Begin your preparation early – Don't wait until the last minute to go scurrying around for books and materials or to find out what the position is all about.
- Prepare continuously – An hour a night for a week is better than an all-night cram session. This has been definitely established. What is more, a night a week for a month will return better dividends than crowding your study into a shorter period of time.
- Locate the place of the exam – You have been sent a notice telling you when and where to report for the examination. If the location is in a different town or otherwise unfamiliar to you, it would be well to inquire the best route and learn something about the building.
- Relax the night before the test – Allow your mind to rest. Do not study at all that night. Plan some mild recreation or diversion; then go to bed early and get a good night's sleep.
- Get up early enough to make a leisurely trip to the place for the test – This way unforeseen events, traffic snarls, unfamiliar buildings, etc. will not upset you.
- Dress comfortably – A written test is not a fashion show. You will be known by number and not by name, so wear something comfortable.

- Leave excess paraphernalia at home – Shopping bags and odd bundles will get in your way. You need bring only the items mentioned in the official notice you received; usually everything you need is provided. Do not bring reference books to the exam. They will only confuse those last minutes and be taken away from you when in the test room.
- Arrive somewhat ahead of time – If because of transportation schedules you must get there very early, bring a newspaper or magazine to take your mind off yourself while waiting.
- Locate the examination room – When you have found the proper room, you will be directed to the seat or part of the room where you will sit. Sometimes you are given a sheet of instructions to read while you are waiting. Do not fill out any forms until you are told to do so; just read them and be prepared.
- Relax and prepare to listen to the instructions
- If you have any physical problem that may keep you from doing your best, be sure to tell the test administrator. If you are sick or in poor health, you really cannot do your best on the exam. You can come back and take the test some other time.

VII. AT THE TEST

The day of the test is here and you have the test booklet in your hand. The temptation to get going is very strong. Caution! There is more to success than knowing the right answers. You must know how to identify your papers and understand variations in the type of short-answer question used in this particular examination. Follow these suggestions for maximum results from your efforts:

1) Cooperate with the monitor

The test administrator has a duty to create a situation in which you can be as much at ease as possible. He will give instructions, tell you when to begin, check to see that you are marking your answer sheet correctly, and so on. He is not there to guard you, although he will see that your competitors do not take unfair advantage. He wants to help you do your best.

2) Listen to all instructions

Don't jump the gun! Wait until you understand all directions. In most civil service tests you get more time than you need to answer the questions. So don't be in a hurry. Read each word of instructions until you clearly understand the meaning. Study the examples, listen to all announcements and follow directions. Ask questions if you do not understand what to do.

3) Identify your papers

Civil service exams are usually identified by number only. You will be assigned a number; you must not put your name on your test papers. Be sure to copy your number correctly. Since more than one exam may be given, copy your exact examination title.

4) Plan your time

Unless you are told that a test is a "speed" or "rate of work" test, speed itself is usually not important. Time enough to answer all the questions will be provided, but this does not mean that you have all day. An overall time limit has been set. Divide the total time (in minutes) by the number of questions to determine the approximate time you have for each question.

5) Do not linger over difficult questions

If you come across a difficult question, mark it with a paper clip (useful to have along) and come back to it when you have been through the booklet. One caution if you do this – be sure to skip a number on your answer sheet as well. Check often to be sure that you have not lost your place and that you are marking in the row numbered the same as the question you are answering.

6) Read the questions

Be sure you know what the question asks! Many capable people are unsuccessful because they failed to *read* the questions correctly.

7) Answer all questions

Unless you have been instructed that a penalty will be deducted for incorrect answers, it is better to guess than to omit a question.

8) Speed tests

It is often better NOT to guess on speed tests. It has been found that on timed tests people are tempted to spend the last few seconds before time is called in marking answers at random – without even reading them – in the hope of picking up a few extra points. To discourage this practice, the instructions may warn you that your score will be "corrected" for guessing. That is, a penalty will be applied. The incorrect answers will be deducted from the correct ones, or some other penalty formula will be used.

9) Review your answers

If you finish before time is called, go back to the questions you guessed or omitted to give them further thought. Review other answers if you have time.

10) Return your test materials

If you are ready to leave before others have finished or time is called, take ALL your materials to the monitor and leave quietly. Never take any test material with you. The monitor can discover whose papers are not complete, and taking a test booklet may be grounds for disqualification.

VIII. EXAMINATION TECHNIQUES

1) Read the general instructions carefully. These are usually printed on the first page of the exam booklet. As a rule, these instructions refer to the timing of the examination; the fact that you should not start work until the signal and must stop work at a signal, etc. If there are any *special* instructions, such as a choice of questions to be answered, make sure that you note this instruction carefully.

2) When you are ready to start work on the examination, that is as soon as the signal has been given, read the instructions to each question booklet, underline any key words or phrases, such as *least, best, outline, describe* and the like. In this way you will tend to answer as requested rather than discover on reviewing your paper that you *listed without describing*, that you selected the *worst* choice rather than the *best* choice, etc.

3) If the examination is of the objective or multiple-choice type – that is, each question will also give a series of possible answers: A, B, C or D, and you are called upon to select the best answer and write the letter next to that answer on your answer paper – it is advisable to start answering each question in turn. There may be anywhere from 50 to 100 such questions in the three or four hours allotted and you can see how much time would be taken if you read through all the questions before beginning to answer any. Furthermore, if you come across a question or group of questions which you know would be difficult to answer, it would undoubtedly affect your handling of all the other questions.

4) If the examination is of the essay type and contains but a few questions, it is a moot point as to whether you should read all the questions before starting to answer any one. Of course, if you are given a choice – say five out of seven and the like – then it is essential to read all the questions so you can eliminate the two that are most difficult. If, however, you are asked to answer all the questions, there may be danger in trying to answer the easiest one first because you may find that you will spend too much time on it. The best technique is to answer the first question, then proceed to the second, etc.

5) Time your answers. Before the exam begins, write down the time it started, then add the time allowed for the examination and write down the time it must be completed, then divide the time available somewhat as follows:
    - If 3-1/2 hours are allowed, that would be 210 minutes. If you have 80 objective-type questions, that would be an average of 2-1/2 minutes per question. Allow yourself no more than 2 minutes per question, or a total of 160 minutes, which will permit about 50 minutes to review.
    - If for the time allotment of 210 minutes there are 7 essay questions to answer, that would average about 30 minutes a question. Give yourself only 25 minutes per question so that you have about 35 minutes to review.

6) The most important instruction is to *read each question* and make sure you know what is wanted. The second most important instruction is to *time yourself properly* so that you answer every question. The third most important instruction is to *answer every question*. Guess if you have to but include something for each question. Remember that you will receive no credit for a blank and will probably receive some credit if you write something in answer to an essay question. If you guess a letter – say "B" for a multiple-choice question – you may have guessed right. If you leave a blank as an answer to a multiple-choice question, the examiners may respect your feelings but it will not add a point to your score. Some exams may penalize you for wrong answers, so in such cases *only*, you may not want to guess unless you have some basis for your answer.

7) Suggestions
    a. Objective-type questions
        1. Examine the question booklet for proper sequence of pages and questions
        2. Read all instructions carefully
        3. Skip any question which seems too difficult; return to it after all other questions have been answered
        4. Apportion your time properly; do not spend too much time on any single question or group of questions

9

5. Note and underline key words – *all, most, fewest, least, best, worst, same, opposite,* etc.
6. Pay particular attention to negatives
7. Note unusual option, e.g., unduly long, short, complex, different or similar in content to the body of the question
8. Observe the use of "hedging" words – *probably, may, most likely,* etc.
9. Make sure that your answer is put next to the same number as the question
10. Do not second-guess unless you have good reason to believe the second answer is definitely more correct
11. Cross out original answer if you decide another answer is more accurate; do not erase until you are ready to hand your paper in
12. Answer all questions; guess unless instructed otherwise
13. Leave time for review

   b. Essay questions
1. Read each question carefully
2. Determine exactly what is wanted. Underline key words or phrases.
3. Decide on outline or paragraph answer
4. Include many different points and elements unless asked to develop any one or two points or elements
5. Show impartiality by giving pros and cons unless directed to select one side only
6. Make and write down any assumptions you find necessary to answer the questions
7. Watch your English, grammar, punctuation and choice of words
8. Time your answers; don't crowd material

8) Answering the essay question

Most essay questions can be answered by framing the specific response around several key words or ideas. Here are a few such key words or ideas:

M's: manpower, materials, methods, money, management
P's: purpose, program, policy, plan, procedure, practice, problems, pitfalls, personnel, public relations
   a. Six basic steps in handling problems:
1. Preliminary plan and background development
2. Collect information, data and facts
3. Analyze and interpret information, data and facts
4. Analyze and develop solutions as well as make recommendations
5. Prepare report and sell recommendations
6. Install recommendations and follow up effectiveness

   b. Pitfalls to avoid
1. *Taking things for granted* – A statement of the situation does not necessarily imply that each of the elements is necessarily true; for example, a complaint may be invalid and biased so that all that can be taken for granted is that a complaint has been registered

2. *Considering only one side of a situation* – Wherever possible, indicate several alternatives and then point out the reasons you selected the best one
3. *Failing to indicate follow up* – Whenever your answer indicates action on your part, make certain that you will take proper follow-up action to see how successful your recommendations, procedures or actions turn out to be
4. *Taking too long in answering any single question* – Remember to time your answers properly

IX. AFTER THE TEST

Scoring procedures differ in detail among civil service jurisdictions although the general principles are the same. Whether the papers are hand-scored or graded by machine we have described, they are nearly always graded by number. That is, the person who marks the paper knows only the number – never the name – of the applicant. Not until all the papers have been graded will they be matched with names. If other tests, such as training and experience or oral interview ratings have been given, scores will be combined. Different parts of the examination usually have different weights. For example, the written test might count 60 percent of the final grade, and a rating of training and experience 40 percent. In many jurisdictions, veterans will have a certain number of points added to their grades.

After the final grade has been determined, the names are placed in grade order and an eligible list is established. There are various methods for resolving ties between those who get the same final grade – probably the most common is to place first the name of the person whose application was received first. Job offers are made from the eligible list in the order the names appear on it. You will be notified of your grade and your rank as soon as all these computations have been made. This will be done as rapidly as possible.

People who are found to meet the requirements in the announcement are called "eligibles." Their names are put on a list of eligible candidates. An eligible's chances of getting a job depend on how high he stands on this list and how fast agencies are filling jobs from the list.

When a job is to be filled from a list of eligibles, the agency asks for the names of people on the list of eligibles for that job. When the civil service commission receives this request, it sends to the agency the names of the three people highest on this list. Or, if the job to be filled has specialized requirements, the office sends the agency the names of the top three persons who meet these requirements from the general list.

The appointing officer makes a choice from among the three people whose names were sent to him. If the selected person accepts the appointment, the names of the others are put back on the list to be considered for future openings.

That is the rule in hiring from all kinds of eligible lists, whether they are for typist, carpenter, chemist, or something else. For every vacancy, the appointing officer has his choice of any one of the top three eligibles on the list. This explains why the person whose name is on top of the list sometimes does not get an appointment when some of the persons lower on the list do. If the appointing officer chooses the second or third eligible, the No. 1 eligible does not get a job at once, but stays on the list until he is appointed or the list is terminated.

X. HOW TO PASS THE INTERVIEW TEST

The examination for which you applied requires an oral interview test. You have already taken the written test and you are now being called for the interview test – the final part of the formal examination.

You may think that it is not possible to prepare for an interview test and that there are no procedures to follow during an interview. Our purpose is to point out some things you can do in advance that will help you and some good rules to follow and pitfalls to avoid while you are being interviewed.

What is an interview supposed to test?

The written examination is designed to test the technical knowledge and competence of the candidate; the oral is designed to evaluate intangible qualities, not readily measured otherwise, and to establish a list showing the relative fitness of each candidate – as measured against his competitors – for the position sought. Scoring is not on the basis of "right" and "wrong," but on a sliding scale of values ranging from "not passable" to "outstanding." As a matter of fact, it is possible to achieve a relatively low score without a single "incorrect" answer because of evident weakness in the qualities being measured.

Occasionally, an examination may consist entirely of an oral test – either an individual or a group oral. In such cases, information is sought concerning the technical knowledges and abilities of the candidate, since there has been no written examination for this purpose. More commonly, however, an oral test is used to supplement a written examination.

Who conducts interviews?

The composition of oral boards varies among different jurisdictions. In nearly all, a representative of the personnel department serves as chairman. One of the members of the board may be a representative of the department in which the candidate would work. In some cases, "outside experts" are used, and, frequently, a businessman or some other representative of the general public is asked to serve. Labor and management or other special groups may be represented. The aim is to secure the services of experts in the appropriate field.

However the board is composed, it is a good idea (and not at all improper or unethical) to ascertain in advance of the interview who the members are and what groups they represent. When you are introduced to them, you will have some idea of their backgrounds and interests, and at least you will not stutter and stammer over their names.

What should be done before the interview?

While knowledge about the board members is useful and takes some of the surprise element out of the interview, there is other preparation which is more substantive. It *is* possible to prepare for an oral interview – in several ways:

1) Keep a copy of your application and review it carefully before the interview

This may be the only document before the oral board, and the starting point of the interview. Know what education and experience you have listed there, and the sequence and dates of all of it. Sometimes the board will ask you to review the highlights of your experience for them; you should not have to hem and haw doing it.

2) Study the class specification and the examination announcement

Usually, the oral board has one or both of these to guide them. The qualities, characteristics or knowledges required by the position sought are stated in these documents. They offer valuable clues as to the nature of the oral interview. For example, if the job involves supervisory responsibilities, the announcement will usually indicate that knowledge of modern supervisory methods and the qualifications of the candidate as a supervisor will be tested. If so, you can expect such questions, frequently in the form of a hypothetical situation which you are expected to solve. NEVER go into an oral without knowledge of the duties and responsibilities of the job you seek.

3) Think through each qualification required

Try to visualize the kind of questions you would ask if you were a board member. How well could you answer them? Try especially to appraise your own knowledge and background in each area, *measured against the job sought*, and identify any areas in which you are weak. Be critical and realistic – do not flatter yourself.

4) Do some general reading in areas in which you feel you may be weak

For example, if the job involves supervision and your past experience has NOT, some general reading in supervisory methods and practices, particularly in the field of human relations, might be useful. Do NOT study agency procedures or detailed manuals. The oral board will be testing your understanding and capacity, not your memory.

5) Get a good night's sleep and watch your general health and mental attitude

You will want a clear head at the interview. Take care of a cold or any other minor ailment, and of course, no hangovers.

What should be done on the day of the interview?

Now comes the day of the interview itself. Give yourself plenty of time to get there. Plan to arrive somewhat ahead of the scheduled time, particularly if your appointment is in the fore part of the day. If a previous candidate fails to appear, the board might be ready for you a bit early. By early afternoon an oral board is almost invariably behind schedule if there are many candidates, and you may have to wait. Take along a book or magazine to read, or your application to review, but leave any extraneous material in the waiting room when you go in for your interview. In any event, relax and compose yourself.

The matter of dress is important. The board is forming impressions about you – from your experience, your manners, your attitude, and your appearance. Give your personal appearance careful attention. Dress your best, but not your flashiest. Choose conservative, appropriate clothing, and be sure it is immaculate. This is a business interview, and your appearance should indicate that you regard it as such. Besides, being well groomed and properly dressed will help boost your confidence.

Sooner or later, someone will call your name and escort you into the interview room. *This is it.* From here on you are on your own. It is too late for any more preparation. But remember, you asked for this opportunity to prove your fitness, and you are here because your request was granted.

What happens when you go in?

The usual sequence of events will be as follows: The clerk (who is often the board stenographer) will introduce you to the chairman of the oral board, who will introduce you to the other members of the board. Acknowledge the introductions before you sit down. Do not be surprised if you find a microphone facing you or a stenotypist sitting by. Oral interviews are usually recorded in the event of an appeal or other review.

Usually the chairman of the board will open the interview by reviewing the highlights of your education and work experience from your application – primarily for the benefit of the other members of the board, as well as to get the material into the record. Do not interrupt or comment unless there is an error or significant misinterpretation; if that is the case, do not hesitate. But do not quibble about insignificant matters. Also, he will usually ask you some question about your education, experience or your present job – partly to get you to start talking and to establish the interviewing "rapport." He may start the actual questioning, or turn it over to one of the other members. Frequently, each member undertakes the questioning on a particular area, one in which he is perhaps most competent, so you can expect each member to participate in the examination. Because time is limited, you may also expect some rather abrupt switches in the direction the questioning takes, so do not be upset by it. Normally, a board member will not pursue a single line of questioning unless he discovers a particular strength or weakness.

After each member has participated, the chairman will usually ask whether any member has any further questions, then will ask you if you have anything you wish to add. Unless you are expecting this question, it may floor you. Worse, it may start you off on an extended, extemporaneous speech. The board is not usually seeking more information. The question is principally to offer you a last opportunity to present further qualifications or to indicate that you have nothing to add. So, if you feel that a significant qualification or characteristic has been overlooked, it is proper to point it out in a sentence or so. Do not compliment the board on the thoroughness of their examination – they have been sketchy, and you know it. If you wish, merely say, "No thank you, I have nothing further to add." This is a point where you can "talk yourself out" of a good impression or fail to present an important bit of information. Remember, *you close the interview yourself.*

The chairman will then say, "That is all, Mr. _____, thank you." Do not be startled; the interview is over, and quicker than you think. Thank him, gather your belongings and take your leave. Save your sigh of relief for the other side of the door.

How to put your best foot forward
Throughout this entire process, you may feel that the board individually and collectively is trying to pierce your defenses, seek out your hidden weaknesses and embarrass and confuse you. Actually, this is not true. They are obliged to make an appraisal of your qualifications for the job you are seeking, and they want to see you in your best light. Remember, they must interview all candidates and a non-cooperative candidate may become a failure in spite of their best efforts to bring out his qualifications. Here are 15 suggestions that will help you:

1) Be natural – Keep your attitude confident, not cocky
If you are not confident that you can do the job, do not expect the board to be. Do not apologize for your weaknesses, try to bring out your strong points. The board is interested in a positive, not negative, presentation. Cockiness will antagonize any board member and make him wonder if you are covering up a weakness by a false show of strength.

2) Get comfortable, but don't lounge or sprawl
Sit erectly but not stiffly. A careless posture may lead the board to conclude that you are careless in other things, or at least that you are not impressed by the importance of the occasion. Either conclusion is natural, even if incorrect. Do not fuss with your clothing, a pencil or an ashtray. Your hands may occasionally be useful to emphasize a point; do not let them become a point of distraction.

3) Do not wisecrack or make small talk
This is a serious situation, and your attitude should show that you consider it as such. Further, the time of the board is limited – they do not want to waste it, and neither should you.

4) Do not exaggerate your experience or abilities

In the first place, from information in the application or other interviews and sources, the board may know more about you than you think. Secondly, you probably will not get away with it. An experienced board is rather adept at spotting such a situation, so do not take the chance.

5) If you know a board member, do not make a point of it, yet do not hide it

Certainly you are not fooling him, and probably not the other members of the board. Do not try to take advantage of your acquaintanceship – it will probably do you little good.

6) Do not dominate the interview

Let the board do that. They will give you the clues – do not assume that you have to do all the talking. Realize that the board has a number of questions to ask you, and do not try to take up all the interview time by showing off your extensive knowledge of the answer to the first one.

7) Be attentive

You only have 20 minutes or so, and you should keep your attention at its sharpest throughout. When a member is addressing a problem or question to you, give him your undivided attention. Address your reply principally to him, but do not exclude the other board members.

8) Do not interrupt

A board member may be stating a problem for you to analyze. He will ask you a question when the time comes. Let him state the problem, and wait for the question.

9) Make sure you understand the question

Do not try to answer until you are sure what the question is. If it is not clear, restate it in your own words or ask the board member to clarify it for you. However, do not haggle about minor elements.

10) Reply promptly but not hastily

A common entry on oral board rating sheets is "candidate responded readily," or "candidate hesitated in replies." Respond as promptly and quickly as you can, but do not jump to a hasty, ill-considered answer.

11) Do not be peremptory in your answers

A brief answer is proper – but do not fire your answer back. That is a losing game from your point of view. The board member can probably ask questions much faster than you can answer them.

12) Do not try to create the answer you think the board member wants

He is interested in what kind of mind you have and how it works – not in playing games. Furthermore, he can usually spot this practice and will actually grade you down on it.

13) Do not switch sides in your reply merely to agree with a board member

Frequently, a member will take a contrary position merely to draw you out and to see if you are willing and able to defend your point of view. Do not start a debate, yet do not surrender a good position. If a position is worth taking, it is worth defending.

14) Do not be afraid to admit an error in judgment if you are shown to be wrong

The board knows that you are forced to reply without any opportunity for careful consideration. Your answer may be demonstrably wrong. If so, admit it and get on with the interview.

15) Do not dwell at length on your present job

The opening question may relate to your present assignment. Answer the question but do not go into an extended discussion. You are being examined for a *new* job, not your present one. As a matter of fact, try to phrase ALL your answers in terms of the job for which you are being examined.

Basis of Rating

Probably you will forget most of these "do's" and "don'ts" when you walk into the oral interview room. Even remembering them all will not ensure you a passing grade. Perhaps you did not have the qualifications in the first place. But remembering them will help you to put your best foot forward, without treading on the toes of the board members.

Rumor and popular opinion to the contrary notwithstanding, an oral board wants you to make the best appearance possible. They know you are under pressure – but they also want to see how you respond to it as a guide to what your reaction would be under the pressures of the job you seek. They will be influenced by the degree of poise you display, the personal traits you show and the manner in which you respond.

ABOUT THIS BOOK

This book contains tests divided into Examination Sections. Go through each test, answering every question in the margin. We have also attached a sample answer sheet at the back of the book that can be removed and used. At the end of each test look at the answer key and check your answers. On the ones you got wrong, look at the right answer choice and learn. Do not fill in the answers first. Do not memorize the questions and answers, but understand the answer and principles involved. On your test, the questions will likely be different from the samples. Questions are changed and new ones added. If you understand these past questions you should have success with any changes that arise. Tests may consist of several types of questions. We have additional books on each subject should more study be advisable or necessary for you. Finally, the more you study, the better prepared you will be. This book is intended to be the last thing you study before you walk into the examination room. Prior study of relevant texts is also recommended. NLC publishes some of these in our Fundamental Series. Knowledge and good sense are important factors in passing your exam. Good luck also helps. So now study this Passbook, absorb the material contained within and take that knowledge into the examination. Then do your best to pass that exam.

EXAMINATION SECTION

EXAMINATION SECTION
TEST 1

DIRECTIONS: Each question or incomplete statement is followed by several suggested answers or completions. Select the one that BEST answers the question or completes the Statement. *PRINT THE LETTER OF THE CORRECT ANSWER IN THE SPACE AT THE RIGHT.*

1. Which of the following substances causes asphalt tile to turn spongy?   1.____

    A. Oil   B. Varnish   C. Water   D. Dust

2. Which of the following would NOT cause asphalt tile to turn yellow?   2.____

    A. A layer of dust   B. Varnish
    C. Lacquer   D. Water

3. Which one of the following is LEAST likely to be an advantage of waxing a floor?   3.____

    A. Helps to make a room quieter
    B. Helps to reduce wear on the floor
    C. Gives a pleasant shine to the floor
    D. Improves the stain resistance of the floor

4. The action of liquid cleaner on a floor with built-up wax is to   4.____

    A. make the wax disappear into the air
    B. turn the wax into little grains that must be swept up in a vacuum cleaner
    C. soften the wax, which has to be scrubbed away and then rinsed off
    D. make the floor waterproof

5. After how many waxings should built-up wax be removed from a floor?
Every   5.____

    A. waxing   B. 3 waxings   C. 6 waxings   D. 12 waxings

6. Manuals on floor cleaning describe methods of cleaning *resilient flooring*.
Which of the following kinds of flooring surfaces is NOT resilient?
_____ tile.   6.____

    A. Cork   B. Asphalt   C. Vinyl   D. Terrazzo

7. In buffing a floor, it is NOT desirable to use a polishing brush because the   7.____

    A. brush will scratch the surface you are trying to polish
    B. strands of the brush fall out easily
    C. brush is often used for other purposes
    D. brush does not usually remove deep scuff marks

8. *Rolling* results when only the upper parts of a wax coat dry, leaving the lower parts wet.
In waxing a floor, this condition comes from   8.____

    A. putting on too thick a coat of wax
    B. putting on too thin a coat of wax
    C. rinsing the floor before applying the wax
    D. leaving soap on the floor before applying the wax

9. After a cork or linoleum floor is installed, how long should you wait before you mop the floor for the FIRST time?   9._____

    A. 1 days   B. 3 days   C. 12 hours   D. 2 weeks

10. On sweeping stairways, you should direct your men to make a practice of sweeping them   10._____

    A. when traffic is heavy so that people can see them working
    B. whenever they have free time during the day
    C. during the morning at a time when traffic is lightest
    D. in the middle of the day when the traffic is medium heavy

11. How often must public corridors be swept?   11._____

    A. Only when a visible amount of dirt piles up
    B. Every day
    C. Once a week
    D. Every three days

12. You should NOT use an oily mop to sweep floor because it   12._____

    A. leaves a sticky film that can catch dust
    B. eats away at the floor like acid
    C. makes the floor completely waterproof
    D. prevents wax from being applied

13. Which of the following would NOT be used on a concrete floor?   13._____

    A. Water base wax   B. Oily sweeping compound
    C. Solvent wax   D. Wire brush

14. You should NOT use an alkaline cleaner on linoleum floors because the cleaner   14._____

    A. will make the floor shine too brightly
    B. makes the linoleum sticky
    C. makes the linoleum crack and curl
    D. costs too much to be practical

15. The BEST way of wet mopping a large floor area is to mop the floor area   15._____

    A. with a circular motion
    B. from side to side or with a figure eight motion
    C. with forward and back strokes
    D. alternate side to side forward and back

16. The type of product to use when cleaning terrazzo floors is   16._____

    A. mild cleaner   B. diluted acid solution
    C. scouring powder   D. paste wax

17. A cleaner was wet mopping an asphalt tile floor. He decided to make the floor as wet as possible.
For him to do this is a

    A. *good* idea, because the more water you use, the cleaner the floor will be
    B. *bad* idea, because water should never be wasted
    C. *good* idea, because the floor will not have to be washed as often
    D. *bad* idea, because the excess water will eventually damage the floor surface

17.____

18. When you wet clean a stairway by hand, you need two buckets.
One of them is for the cleaning solution, and the other one is used for

    A. extra ammonia for cleaning
    B. rinsing, and should be filled with clean water
    C. putting out fires, and should be filled with sand
    D. storage of equipment

18.____

19. The cleaning of stairways is USUALLY scheduled to be done with

    A. corridor cleaning   B. sidewalk cleaning
    C. incinerator work   D. move-outs

19.____

20. *Dry cleaning* in relation to a building refers to

    A. a reconditioning process that restores the appearance of a floor and protects the surface by buffing
    B. dusting of a wall area with specially treated cloth in order to produce a sheen
    C. patch waxing of a floor with a powdered wax compound
    D. dry mopping only of a floor area

20.____

Questions 21-24.

DIRECTION: Questions 21 through 24, inclusive, are to be answered SOLELY on the basis of the following paragraph.

All cleaning agents and supplies should be kept in a central storeroom which should be kept locked and only the custodian, store keeper, and foreman should have keys. Shelving should be provided for the smaller items, while barrels containing scouring powder or other bulk material should be set on the floor or on special cradles. Each compartment in the shelves should be marked plainly and only the item indicated stored therein. Each barrel should also be marked plainly. It may also be desirable to keep special items such as electric lamps, flashlight batteries, etc. in a locked cabinet or separate room to which only the custodian and the night building foreman have keys.

21. According to the above paragraph, scouring powder

    A. should be kept on shelves
    B. comes in one-pound cans
    C. should be kept in a locked cabinet
    D. is a bulk material

21.____

22. According to the above paragraph,

    A. the storekeeper should not be entrusted with the safekeeping of lightbulbs
    B. flashlight batteries should be stored in barrels
    C. the central storeroom should be kept locked
    D. only special items should be stored under lock and key

22.____

23. According to the above paragraph,

    A. each shelf compartment should contain at least four different Items
    B. barrels must be stored in cradles
    C. all items stored should be in marked compartments
    D. crates of lightbulbs should be stored in cradles

23.____

24. As used In the above paragraph, the word *cradle* means a

    A. dolly   B. support
    C. doll's bed   D. hand truck

24.____

25. The material recommended for removing blood or fruit stains from concrete is

    A. soft soap   B. neatsfoot oil
    C. oxalic acid   D. ammonia

25.____

KEY (CORRECT ANSWER)

1.	A		11.	B
2.	A		12.	A
3.	A		13.	B
4.	C		14.	C
5.	C		15.	B
6.	D		16.	A
7.	D		17.	D
8.	A		18.	B
9.	B		19.	A
10.	C		20.	A

21.	D
22.	C
23.	C
24.	B
25.	D

TEST 2

DIRECTIONS: Each question or incomplete statement Is followed by several suggested answers or completions. Select the one that BEST answers the question or completes the statement. *PRINT THE LETTER OF THE CORRECT ANSWER IN THE SPACE AT THE RIGHT.*

1. The wall surface which does NOT have to be washed from the bottom up to avoid streaking is a(n) _____ wall.   1.____

    A. semi-gloss painted   B. enamel painted
    C. glazed tile   D. unglazed tile

2. The one of the following practices which is GENERALLY recommended to prolong the useful life of a corn broom is   2.____

    A. soaking a new broom overnight before using it for the first time to remove brittle-ness
    B. storing the broom with the tips of the straws resting on the floor to keep the edges even
    C. keeping the straws moistened when sweeping
    D. storing the broom in a warm humid enclosure to prevent drying of the bristles

3. While a cleaner is sweeping the public corridors and stairways, he notices some crayon marks on walls and stains on the floors.
He should   3.____

    A. stop sweeping and remove the stains immediately
    B. finish sweeping and then return to remove the stains
    C. make note of the marks and stains in his building and remove them once a month
    D. make a note of the marks and stains and report them to the superintendent so that the cause can be eliminated before the stains are removed

4. When transporting the equipment required for mopping stairhalls and corridors, a cleaner should NOT   4.____

    A. attempt to do it alone
    B. carry water in the pails because spillage may cause a tenant to slip and fall
    C. use the elevator
    D. carry the equipment in both hands when climbing stairs

5. A cleaner should apply washing solution to a portion of a painted wall and should rinse the same area before applying the solution to another area.
In order to allow sufficient time for the solution to take effect on the soil, the area covered each time should be APPROXIMATELY _____ square feet.   5.____

    A. 20   B. 60   C. 160   D. 600

6. Asphalt tile floors should be maintained by coating them with   6.____

    A. water emulsion wax   B. paste wax
    C. oil emulsion wax   D. neatsfoot oil

7. The broom with which a cleaner should sweep an asphalt-paved playground is the _____ broom.

    A. hair   B. corn   C. garage   D. Scotch

8. The central vacuum cleaning system should be cleaned

    A. weekly   B. twice weekly
    C. daily   D. when necessary

9. The FIRST thing a window cleaner should do is

    A. test window bolts
    B. see that cleaning tools are good
    C. cheak window belt
    D. nit lean too heavily on glass

10. During a shortage of custodial help in a public building, the cleaning task which will probably receive LEAST attention is

    A. picking up sweepings   B. emptying ashtrays
    C. washing walls   D. dust-mopping offices

11. Of the following substances commonly used on floors, the MOST flammable is

    A. resin-based floor finish   B. floor sealer
    C. water emulsion wax   D. trisodium phosphate

12. The MOST effective method for cleaning badly soiled carpeting is

    A. wet shampooing   B. vacuum cleaning
    C. dry shampooing   D. wire brushing

13. Painted walls and ceilings should be brushed down

    A. daily
    B. weekly
    C. every month, especially during the winter
    D. two or three times a year

14. If an asphalt tile floor become excessively dirty, the method of cleaning should include

    A. the use of kerosene or benzine as a solvent
    B. the use of a solution of modified laundry soda
    C. sanding down the spotted areas with a sanding machine on the wet floor
    D. use of a light oil and treated mop

15. To remove light stains from marble walls, the BEST method is to

    A. use steel wool and a scouring powder, then rinse with clear warm water
    B. was the stained area with a dilute acid solution
    C. sand down the spot first, then wash with mild soap solution
    D. wet marble first, then scrub with mild soap solution using a soft fiber brush

16. To rid a toilet room of objectionable odors, the PROPER method is to 16.____

  A. spread some chloride of lime on the floor
  B. place deodorizer cubes in a box hung on the wall
  C. wash the floor with hot water containing a little kerosene
  D. wash the floor with hot water into which some disinfectant has been poured

17. Toilet rooms, to be cleaned properly, should be swept 17.____

  A. daily
  B. and mopped daily
  C. daily and mopped twice a week
  D. daily and mopped thoroughly at the end of the

18. In waxing a floor, it is usually BEST to 18.____

  A. start the waxing under stationary furniture and then do the aisles
  B. pour the wax on the floor, spreading it under the desks with a wax mop
  C. remove the old wax coat before rewaxing
  D. wet mop the floor after the second coat has dried to obtain a high polish

19. Of the following, the MOST important reason why a wet mop should NOT be wrung out 19.____
by hand is that

  A. the strings of the mop will be damaged by hand-wringing
  B. sharp objects picked up by the mop may injure the hands
  C. the mop cannot be made dry enough by hand-wringing
  D. fine dirt will become embedded in the strings of the mop

20. When a painted wall is washed by hand, the wall should be washed from the 20.____

  A. top down, with a soaking wet sponge
  B. bottom up, with a soaking wet sponge
  C. top down, with a damp sponge
  D. bottom up, with a damp sponge

21. When a painted wall is brushed with a clean lambswool duster, the duster should be 21.____
drawn _____ with a _____ pressure.

  A. downward; light   B. upward; light
  C. downward; firm   D. upward; firm

22. The one of the following terms which BEST describes the size of a floor brush is 22.____

  A. 72 cubic inch   B. 32 ounce
  C. 24 inch   D. 10 square foot

23. Terrazzo floors should be mopped periodically with a(n) 23.____

  A. acid solution
  B. neutral detergent in warm water
  C. mop treated with kerosene
  D. strong alkaline solution

24. The MAIN reason why the handle of a reversible floor brush should be shifted from one side of the brush block to the opposite side is to

    A. change the angle at which the brush sweeps the floor
    B. give equal wear to both sides of the brush
    C. permit the brush to sweep hard-to-reach areas
    D. make it easier to sweep backward

24.____

25. When a long corridor is swept with a floor brush, it is good practice to

    A. push the brush with moderately long strokes and flick it after each stroke
    B. press on the brush and push it the whole length of the corridor in one sweep
    C. pull the brush inward with short, brisk strokes
    D. sweep across rather than down the length of the corridor

25.____

KEY (CORRECT ANSWERS)

1.	C	11.	B
2.	A	12.	A
3.	B	13.	D
4.	D	14.	D
5.	C	15.	D
6.	A	16.	D
7.	C	17.	B
8.	B	18.	A
9.	C	19.	B
10.	C	20.	D

21.	A
22.	C
23.	B
24.	B
25.	A

TEST 3

DIRECTIONS: Each question or incomplete statement is followed by several suggested answers or completions. Select the one that BEST answers the question or completes the Statement. *PRINT THE LETTER OF THE CORRECT ANSWER IN THE SPACE AT THE RIGHT.*

1. The MOST common cause of slipperiness of a terrazzo floor after it has been washed is the

    A. failure to rinse the floor clean of the cleaning agent
    B. destruction of the floor seal by the cleaning agent
    C. incomplete removal of dirt from the floor
    D. use of oil in the cleaning process

1.____

2. When electric lighting fixtures are washed, a precaution that should be observed is:

    A. The metal part of the fixture should be washed with a warm mild ammonia solution
    B. Holding screws of the glass globe should be loosened about one-half turn after they have all been applied to the cleaned globe
    C. Trisodium phosphate should not be used in washing glass globes because it dulls the glass
    D. Chain links of the fixture should be loosened to enable removal of the entire fixture for cleaning

2.____

3. A cleaner will make the BEST impression on the office staff if he

    A. impresses them with the importance of his job
    B. says little and is cold and distant
    C. is easy-going and good-natured
    D. is courteous and performs his duties with as little delay as possible

3.____

4. If it is necessary to wash stairways, this should be done during the

    A. day   B. night
    C. weekend   D. morning rush hour

4.____

5. A detergent is GENERALLY used in

    A. waterproofing walls   B. killing crabgrass
    C. cleaning floor and walls   D. exterminating rodents

5.____

6. Many new products are used in new buildings for floors, walls, and other surfaces. A cleaner should determine the BEST procedure to be used to clean such new surfaces by

    A. referring to the manual of procedures
    B. obtaining information on the cleaning procedure from the manufacturer
    C. asking the advice of the mechanics who installed the new material
    D. asking the district supervisor how to clean the surfaces

6.____

7. A window cleaner should carefully examine his safety belt

    A. once a week
    B. before he puts it on each time
    C. once a month
    D. once before he enters a building

7.____

8. One of your cleaners was injured as a result of slipping on an oily floor. This type of accident is MOST likely due to

    A. defective equipment
    B. the physical condition of the cleaner
    C. failure to use proper safety appliances
    D. poor housekeeping

8.____

9. For wet mopping the floor of a corridor by hand, the MINIMUM number of pails needed is

    A. one   B. two   C. three   D. four

9.____

10. A comparison of wet mopping by hand with scrubbing by hand indicates that mopping

    A. needs more cleaning solution
    B. is more time-consuming
    C. requires twice as much water
    D. is less effective on hardened soil

10.____

11. Chrome fixtures should be cleaned by

    A. using a mild soap solution then polishing with a soft cloth
    B. dusting lightly, then wax with an oil base wax
    C. polishing with a scouring pad
    D. washing with a solution of water and ammonia, then rinsing with a detergent

11.____

12. The BEST way for a building custodian to tell if the night cleaners have done their work well is to check

    A. on how much cleaning material has been used
    B. on how much wastepaper was collected
    C. the building for cleanliness
    D. the floor mops to see if they are still wet

12.____

13. THe one of the following items which ordinarily requires the MOST time to wash is a(n)

    A. 5 ft x 10 ft. Venetian blind
    B. 4 ft fluorescent fixture
    C. incandescent fixture
    D. 5 ft x 10 ft ceramic tile floor

13.____

14. A broom that has been properly used should GENERALLY be replaced after

    A. it has been used for one month
    B. its bristles have been worn down by more than one-third of their original length
    C. it has been used for two months
    D. its bristles have been worn down by more than two-thirds of their original length

14.____

15. Carbon tetrachloride is NOT recommended for cleaning purposes because of

    A. the poisonous nature of its fumes
    B. its limited cleaning value
    C. the damaging effects it has on equipment
    D. the difficulty of application

15.____

16. Proper care of floor brushes includes   16.____

    A. washing brushes daily after each use with warm soap solution
    B. dipping brushes in kerosene periodically to remove dirt
    C. washing with warm soap solution at least once a month
    D. avoiding contact with soap or soda solutions to prevent drying of bristles

17. Of the following, the cleaning assignment which you would LEAST prefer to have per-   17.____
    formed during school hours is

    A. sweeping of corridors and stairs
    B. cleaning and polishing of brass fixtures
    C. cleaning toilets
    D. dusting of offices, halls, and special rooms

18. A cleaning detergent is composed of   18.____

    A. cleaning acids   B. salts
    C. sodium compounds   D. alkaline compounds

19. Neatsfoot oil is commonly used to   19.____

    A. oil light machinery
    B. prepare sweeping compound
    C. clean metal fixtures
    D. treat leather-covered chairs

20. The one of the following terms which BEST describes the size of a floor mop is   20.____

    A. 10 quart   B. 32 ounce
    C. 24 inch O.D.   D. 10 square feet

21. Cleaners will USUALLY be motivated to do a good job by a custodian who   21.____

    A. lets them get away with poor performance
    B. treats them fairly
    C. treats some of them more favorably than others
    D. lets them take a nap in the afternoon

22. When changing brushes on a scrubbing machine, of the following, the FIRST step to   22.____
    take is to

    A. lock the switch in the *off* position
    B. be sure the power cable electric plug supplying the machine is disconnected from
       the wall outlet
    C. place the machine on top of the positioned brushes
    D. dip the brushes in water

23. The BEST method or tool to use for cleaning dust from an unplastered cinderblock wall is   23.____

    A. a tampico brush with stock cleaning solution
    B. a vacuum cleaner
    C. water under pressure from hose and nozzle
    D. a feather duster

24. The BEST reason for cleaning lightbulbs is   24.____

    A. the bulb willlast longer
    B. removing dust
    C. obtaining optimum light
    D. preventing electrical shock

25. Effluorescence may BEST be removed from brickwork by washing with a solution of   25.____
_____ acid.

    A. muriatic   B. citric   C. carbonic   D. nitric

KEY (CORRECT ANSWERS)

1.	A	11.	A
2.	B	12.	C
3.	D	13.	A
4.	C	14.	B
5.	C	15.	A
6.	B	16.	C
7.	B	17.	C
8.	D	18.	C
9.	B	19.	D
10.	D	20.	B

21.	B
22.	B
23.	B
24.	C
25.	A

EXAMINATION SECTION
TEST 1

DIRECTIONS: Each question or incomplete statement is followed by several suggested answers or completions. Select the one that BEST answers the question or completes the statement. *PRINT THE LETTER OF THE CORRECT ANSWER IN THE SPACE AT THE RIGHT.*

1. Employees should be familiar with the rules and regulations governing their jobs *mainly* to

    A. eliminate overtime
    B. justify mistakes
    C. pass promotion examinations
    D. perform their duties properly

1.____

2. When summoning an ambulance for an injured person, it is MOST important to give the

    A. name of the injured person
    B. nature of the injuries
    C. cause of the accident
    D. location of the injured person

2.____

3. The *most likely* cause of accidents involving minor injuries is

    A. careless work practices
    B. lack of safety devices
    C. inferior equipment and material
    D. insufficient safety posters

3.____

4. When you are newly assigned as a helper to an experienced maintainer, he is *most likely* to give you good training if your attitude is that

    A. he is responsible for your progress
    B. you have the basic knowledge but lack the details
    C. you need the benefit of his experience
    D. he should do the jobs where little is to be learned

4.____

5. A sheet metal plate has been cut in the form of a right triangle with sides of 5, 12, and 13 inches. The area of this plate is, in square inches,

    A. 30   B. 32 1/2   C. 60   D. 78

5.____

6. The side support for steps or stairs is called a

    A. ledger board   B. runner
    C. stringer   D. riser

6.____

7. In an accident report, the information which may be MOST useful in DECREASING the recurrence of similar type accidents is the

    A. extent of injuries sustained
    B. time the accident happened
    C. number of people involved
    D. cause of the accident

7.____

8. The circumference of a circle is given by the formula $C = \pi D$, where C is the circumference, D is the diameter and π is about 3 1/7. If a coil of 15 turns of steel cable has an average diameter of 20 inches, the TOTAL length of cable, in feet, on the coil is NEAREST to

    A. 5   B. 78   C. 550   D. 943

8.____

9. In order to determine if a surface is truly horizontal, it should be checked with a

    A. carpenter's square   B. plumb bob
    C. steel rule   D. spirit level

9.____

10. A steel beam that is supported at one end on a masonry wall will *generally* be provided with a steel bearing plate under this end in order to

    A. protect the beam from any corrosive action of the masonry
    B. prevent the wall from being injured by any failure of the beam
    C. spread the load from the beam over a wider area of the wall
    D. prevent any rocking motion of the beam on the wall

10.____

11. Before a newly riveted connection can be approved, the rivets should be struck with a light hammer in order to

    A. improve the shape of the rivet heads
    B. knock off any rust or burnt metal
    C. detect any loose rivets
    D. give the rivets a tighter fit

11.____

12. Wall sheathing can be installed either diagonally or horizontally on the studs. When installed diagonally, the wall is

    A. cheaper   B. smoother
    C. more weatherproof   D. more rigid

12.____

13. The measurements of a poured concrete foundation shows that 54 cubic feet of concrete have been placed. If payment for this concrete is to be on the basic of cubic yards, the 54 cubic feet must be

    A. multiplied by 27   B. multiplied by 3
    C. divided by 27   D. divided by 3

13.____

14. The two materials which have been used to the GREATEST extent for the construction of the subway system are

    A. brick and steel   B. steel and concrete
    C. wood and steel   D. wood and concrete

14.____

15. The spacing along the track from one subway column to the next is *generally* about _____ feet.

    A. 2   B. 5   C. 25   D. 50

15.____

QUESTIONS 16-25.

Questions 16 to 25 inclusive in Column I are articles or terms used in structure maintenance and repair work, each of which is associated *primarily* (though not exclusively) with one of the trade specialties listed in Column II. For each article or term in Column I, select the trade specialty from Column II in which it is in greatest use. Indicate in the correspondingly numbered row the letter preceding your selected trade specialty.

Column I (Articles or Terms)	Column II (Trade Specialities)	
16. Drift pin	A. Carpentry	16._____
17. Studding	B. Masonry	17._____
18. Elbow	C. Ironwork	18._____
19. Header course	D. Plumbing	19._____
20. Dowel		20._____
21. Screeding		21._____
22. Cleanout		22._____
23. Air jam		23._____
24. Curing		24._____
25. Mortise and tenon		25._____

KEY (CORRECT ANSWERS)

1.	D	11.	C
2.	D	12.	D
3.	A	13.	C
4.	C	14.	B
5.	A	15.	B
6.	C	16.	C
7.	D	17.	A
8.	B	18.	D
9.	D	19.	B
10.	C	20.	A

21.	B
22.	D
23.	C
24.	B
25.	A

TEST 2

DIRECTIONS: Each question or incomplete statement is followed by several suggested answers or completions. Select the one that BEST answers the question or completes the statement. *PRINT THE LETTER OF THE CORRECT ANSWER IN THE SPACE AT THE RIGHT.*

1. A foreman reprimands a helper for walking across the subway tracks unnecessarily in violation of the rules and regulations. The BEST reaction of the helper in this situation is to   1.___

    A. tell the foreman that he was careful and that he did not take any chances
    B. keep quiet and accept the criticism
    C. explain that he took this action to save time
    D. demand that the foreman show him the rule he violated

2. The helper who would probably be rated HIGHEST by his supervisor is the one who   2.___

    A. listens to instruction and carries them out
    B. never lets the maintainer to whom he is assigned do any heavy lifting
    C. asks many questions about the work
    D. makes many suggestions on work procedures

3. If a co-worker is not breathing after receiving an electric shock but is no longer in contact with the electricity, it is MOST important for you to   3.___

    A. avoid moving him
    B. wrap the victim in a blanket
    C. force him to take hot liquids
    D. start artificial respiration promptly

4. Good practice requires that the end of a pipe to be installed in a plumbing system be reamed to remove the inside burr after it has been cut to length. The purpose of this reaming is to   4.___

    A. remove loose rust
    B. finish the pipe accurately to length
    C. restore the original inside diameter of the pipe at the end
    D. make the threading of the pipe easier

5. A box contains an equal number of iron and brass castings. Each iron casting weighs 2 pounds and each brass casting one pound. If the box contents weigh 240 lbs., the number of iron pieces in the box is   5.___

    A. 160   B. 120   C. 80   D. 40

6. The roofs of stations on the elevated sections of rail are *generally* covered with   6.___

    A. sheet metal   B. asbestos shingles
    C. tiles   D. tar paper

7. Where wide train steps are provided with a center dividing railing, the railing is *usually* constructed of   7.___

    A. angle irons   B. steel pipe
    C. sheet metal panels   D. wrought iron

8. If the feet of a ladder are found to be resting on a slightly uneven surface, it would be BEST to

    A. move the ladder to an entirely different location
    B. even up the feet of the ladder with a small wedge
    C. get two men to bolster the ladder while it is being climbed
    D. get another ladder that is more suitable to the conditions

8.____

9. It would be POOR practice to hold a piece of wood in your hands or lap while you are tightening a screw in the wood because

    A. the wood would probably split
    B. sufficient leverage cannot be obtained
    C. the screwdriver may bend
    D. you might injure yourself

9.____

10. A mixture of cement, sand, and water is called

    A. hydrated lime
    C. hydrated cement
    B. plain concrete
    D. mortar

10.____

11. A gauge of a nail indicates the

    A. length of the shank
    C. thickness of the head
    B. diameter of the head
    D. diameter of the shank

11.____

12. If a man on a job has to report an accident to the office by telephone, he should request the name of the person taking the call and also note the time. The reason for this precaution is to fix responsibility for the

    A. entire handling of the accident thereafter
    B. accuracy of the report
    C. recording of the report
    D. preparation of the final written report

12.____

13. Employees of the transit system whose work requires them to enter upon the tracks in the subway are warned NOT to wear loose fitting clothes. The MOST important reason for this warning is that loose fitting clothes may

    A. tear more easily than snug fitting clothes
    B. give insufficient protection against subway dust
    C. catch on some projection of a passing train
    D. interfere when the men are using heavy tools

13.____

14. An effective material frequently used for preserving wood from weathering and decay is

    A. creosote
    C. spelter
    B. zinc chloride
    D. pumice

14.____

15. The MOST important reason for roping off a work area on a subway station is to

    A. prevent transit delays
    B. protect the public
    C. protect the work gang
    D. prevent the work gang from being distracted by the public

15.____

16. Shoes with sponge rubber soles should NOT be worn in working areas *mainly* because they

    A. are not waterproof
    B. are easily punctured by steel objects
    C. do not keep the feet warm
    D. wear out too quickly

17. The area (in square inches) of the plate shown is

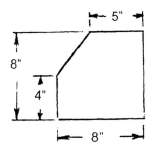

    A. 32   B. 52   C. 58   D. 64

18. In the wood frame shown, whose corners are all square, the total length of one-inch board is _____ inches.

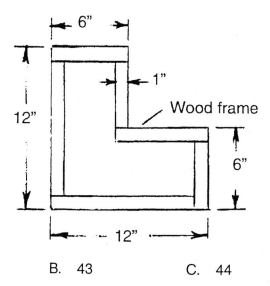

Wood frame

    A. 42   B. 43   C. 44   D. 45

19. On the curved metal sheet, the distance X is, in inches,

19.____

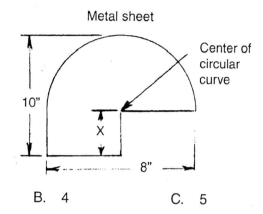

A. 3   B. 4   C. 5   D. 6

20. The number of feet of wire fencing needed to divide the area shown into four completely fenced-in square sections, all equal in area, would be

20.____

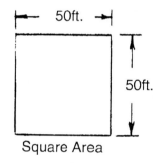

A. 2500   B. 300   C. 200   D. 100

21. When floor beams are to be supported by nailing to vertical supports, then the STRONGEST arrangement would be provided by the method shown in sketch No.

21.____

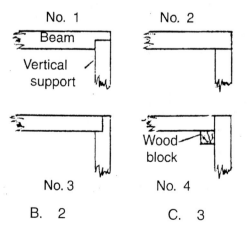

A. 1   B. 2   C. 3   D. 4

22. The weight "W" is to be raised as shown by attaching the pull rope to a truck. If the weight is to be raised 8 feet, the truck will have to move _____ feet.   22.____

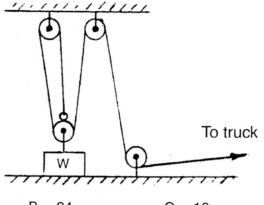

To truck

A. 32   B. 24   C. 16   D. 8

23. Four plots of ground of equal area are as shown. It is proposed to use chain-link fencing to fence in the four plots. The LEAST amount of fencing would be needed for plot No.   23.____

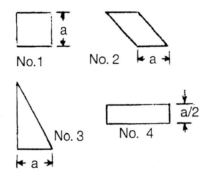

A. 1   B. 2   C. 3   D. 4

24. The area of the shaded portion of the circle shown is found by multiplying one-fourth of the square of the diameter, D, by 22/7 and by   24.____

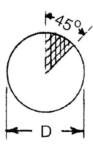

A. 1/8   B. 1/6   C. 1/4   D. 1/3

25. The open-top tin box shown at the right can be made by bending along the dotted lines of   25.____
    the flat cut sheet marked

Tin Box

A. 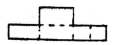   B.

C.   D.

KEY (CORRECT ANSWERS)

1.	B		11.	D
2.	A		12.	C
3.	D		13.	C
4.	C		14.	A
5.	C		15.	B
6.	A		16.	B
7.	B		17.	C
8.	B		18.	C
9.	D		19.	D
10.	D		20.	B

21.	B
22.	B
23.	A
24.	A
25.	D

TEST 3

DIRECTIONS: Each question or incomplete statement is followed by several suggested answers or completions. Select the one that BEST answers the question or completes the statement. *PRINT THE LETTER OF THE CORRECT ANSWER IN THE SPACE AT THE RIGHT.*

1. In MOST cases, the logical and proper source from which you should FIRST seek explanation of a transit rule you do not understand would be the

    A. helper who has an assignment similar to yours
    B. maintainer with whom you are assigned to work
    C. head of your department
    D. transit authority

1.____

2. In case of accident, employees who witnessed the accident are required by the rules to make individual written reports on prescribed forms as soon as possible. The MOST logical reason for requiring such individual reports rather than a single joint report signed by all witnesses is that the individual reports are

    A. *less* likely to be lost at the same time
    B. *more* likely to result in reducing the number of accidents
    C. *less* likely to contain unnecessary information
    D. *more* likely to give the complete picture

2.____

3. The pipe that is MOST likely to break if it is dropped is one made from

    A. soft steel   B. wrought iron
    C. aluminum   D. cast iron

3.____

4. A nominal 6" x 8" wood timber as normally obtained is *actually*

    A. a full 6" thick and a full 8" deep
    B. more than 6" thick and more than 8" deep
    C. less than 6" thick and less than 8" deep
    D. more than 6" thick but less than 8" deep

4.____

5. A serious safety hazard occurs when a

    A. hardened steel hammer is used to strike a hardened steel surface
    B. soft iron hammer is used to strike a hardened steel surface
    C. hardened steel hammer is used to strike a soft iron surface
    D. soft iron hammer is used to strike a soft iron surface

5.____

6. When an emergency exit door set in the sidewalk is being opened from inside the subway, the door should be opened slowly to avoid

    A. injury to pedestrian
    B. making unnecessary noise
    C. a sudden rush of air from the street
    D. damage to the sidewalk

6.____

7. The MAIN purpose of the periodic inspections of transit facilities and equipment that are made by the maintainers is *probably* to

7.____

    A. encourage the men to take better care of these facilities and equipment
    B. keep the maintainers busy during otherwise slack periods
    C. discover minor faults before they develop into more serious conditions
    D. make the men more familiar with these facilities and equipment

8. A rule of the transit system prohibits the use of transit system telephones for personal calls. The MOST important reason for this rule is that the added personal calls   8._____

    A. increase telephone maintenance
    B. require more operators
    C. tie up telephones which may be urgently needed for company business
    D. waste company time

9. Bricks are usually so placed in a brick wall that joints between bricks in any row do not line up with joints in the row immediately above and the one immediately below. The MAIN purpose of this staggering of bricks is to   9._____

    A. obtain a pleasing design
    B. make it easier to keep the successive rows level when laying the bricks
    C. prevent rain water from running in channels down the wall
    D. form a firmer wall

10. If you feel that one of your co-workers is not doing his share of the work, your BEST procedure is to   10._____

    A. increase your own output as a good example
    B. take no action and continue to do your job properly
    C. reduce your work output to bring this matter to a head
    D. point this out to the foreman

11. Maintenance workers of the transit system are required to report defective equipment to their superiors even when the maintenance of the particular equipment is handled by another bureau. The purpose of this rule is to   11._____

    A. reward those who keep their eyes open
    B. punish employees who do not do their jobs
    C. have repairs made before serious trouble occurs
    D. keep employees on their toes

12. When you are FIRST appointed as a helper and are assigned to work with a maintainer, he will *probably* expect you to   12._____

    A. pay close attention to instructions
    B. do very little work
    C. make plenty of mistakes
    D. do all of the unpleasant work

13. Concrete will crack MOST easily when it is subject to   13._____

    A. compression   B. bearing   C. bonding   D. tension

14. When marking and sawing a timber to a desired length, it is GOOD practice to mark   14._____

A. slightly smaller than the length and saw just outside the line on the waste side
B. the exact length and cut just outside the line on the waste side
C. the exact length and cut on the line
D. slightly larger than the length and cut on the line

15. From your knowledge and observation of the subway, the logical reason that certain employees who work on the tracks carry small parts in fiber pails rather than steel pails is that fiber pails

15.____

A. cannot be dented by rough usage
B. do not conduct electricity
C. are stronger
D. cannot rust

16. Maintenance workers whose duties require them to work on the tracks generally work in pairs. The LEAST likely of the following possible reasons for this practice is that

16.____

A. the men can help each other in case of accident
B. it protects against vandalism
C. some of the work requires two men
D. there is usually too much equipment for one man to carry

17. In order to repair a leaky faucet, it would be BEST to FIRST replace the

17.____

A. washer   B. spindle   C. bonnet   D. seat

QUESTIONS 18-25.
Questions 18 to 25 refer to the figures below.

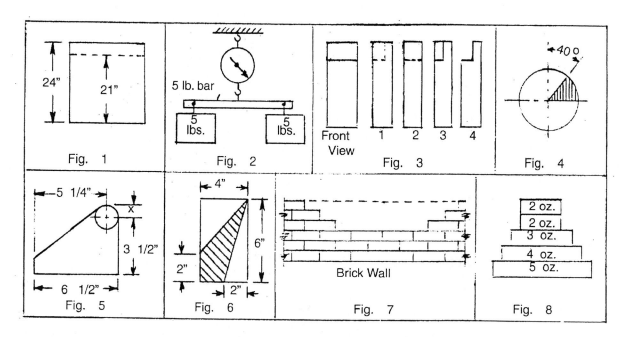

18. Fig. 1 shows a water tank having a total capacity of 120 gallons, which is partially filled. If 60 gallons are drained, the NEW water level will be

18.____

A. 16"   B. 13"   C. 9"   D. 7"

19. In Fig. 2, which shows a balanced bar, the weighing scale will read *approximately*   19.____

    A. zero   B. 5 lbs.   C. 10 lbs.   D. 15 lbs.

20. Fig. 3 shows a front view of a steel piece. The CORRECT SIDE view is No.   20.____

    A. 1   B. 2   C. 3   D. 4

21. Fig. 4 shows a shaded sector on a circular metal sheet. The MAXIMUM number of such sectors which can be cut from the sheet is   21.____

    A. 7   B. 8   C. 9   D. 10

22. In Fig. 5, dimension "X" is   22.____

    A. 1 1/4"   B. 1 3/4"   C. 2"   D. 2 1/2"

23. In Fig. 6, the area in square inches of the shaded portion of the rectangle is   23.____

    A. 10   B. 14   C. 24   D. 28

24. In Fig. 7, the number of full-size bricks required to complete the brick wall to the dotted line is   24.____

    A. 7   B. 9   C. 12   D. 15

25. Using only the balance weights shown in Fig. 8, the LEAST number of weights needed for a scale requiring 3/4 pounds of weights to balance is   25.____

    A. 5   B. 4   C. 3   D. 2

KEY (CORRECT ANSWERS)

1.	B		11.	C
2.	D		12.	A
3.	D		13.	D
4.	C		14.	B
5.	A		15.	B
6.	A		16.	B
7.	C		17.	A
8.	C		18.	C
9.	D		19.	D
10.	B		20.	D

21.	A
22.	A
23.	A
24.	C
25.	C

TEST 4

DIRECTIONS: Each question or incomplete statement is followed by several suggested answers or completions. Select the one that BEST answers the question or completes the statement. *PRINT THE LETTER OF THE CORRECT ANSWER IN THE SPACE AT THE RIGHT.*

1. The MAIN reason for not permitting more than one person to work on a ladder at the same time is that

    A. the ladder might get overloaded
    B. several persons on the ladder might obstruct each other
    C. time would be lost going up and down the ladder
    D. several persons could not all face the ladder at one time

1.____

2. Safety on the job is BEST assured by

    A. keeping alert
    B. working only with new tools
    C. working very slowly
    D. avoiding the necessity for working overtime

2.____

3. The structural steel member that is used to support a wall over a door or window opening is called a

    A. sill   B. lintel   C. stud   D. plate

3.____

4. A mixture of cement and water is referred to as _____ cement.

    A. neat   B. Portland   C. fine   D. hydrated

4.____

5. To secure the proper angle for resting a 12-foot ladder against a wall, the ladder should be so inclined that the distance between the bottom of the ladder and the wall is _____ feet.

    A. 2   B. 3   C. 4   D. 5

5.____

QUESTIONS 6-25.
Questions 6-25 refer to the use of tools shown below. Refer to these tools when answering these questions.

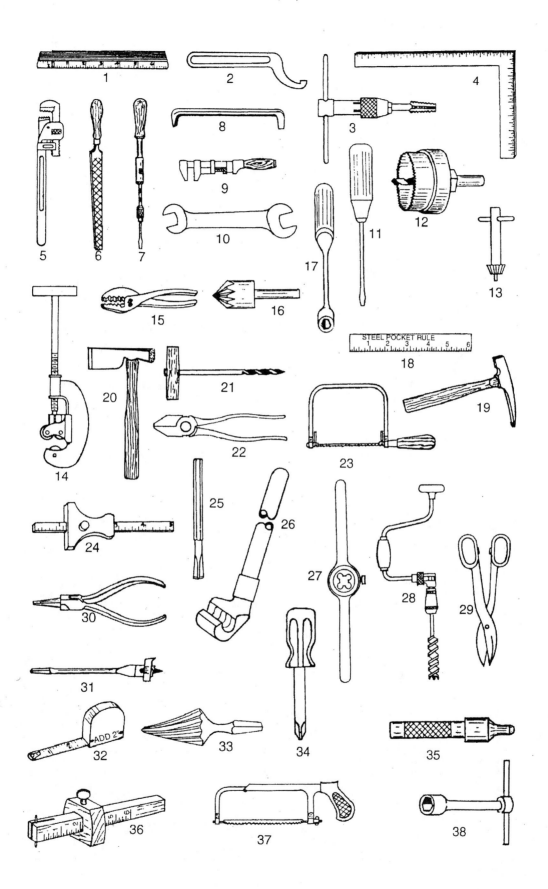

6. Tool number 38 is properly called a(n) _____ wrench.　　　　　　　　　6.____

    A. box   B. open-end   C. socket   D. tool

7. Two tools which are used for cutting large circular holes in thin sheets are numbers　　7.____

    A. 12 and 31   B. 28 and 33   C. 12 and 28   D. 31 and 33

8. If there is a possible danger of electric shock when you are taking measurements, it   8.____
would be BEST to use number

    A. 1   B. 4   C. 18   D. 32

9. A 1/2-inch steel pipe is *preferably* cut with number   9.____

    A. 14   B. 23   C. 27   D. 29

10. A nut for a #8 machine screw should be tightened using number   10.____

    A. 9   B. 15   C. 17   D. 38

11. The hexagon nut for a 1/2-inch diameter machine bolt should be tightened using number   11.____

    A. 5   B. 10   C. 22   D. 26

12. If a small piece must be chipped off a brick in order to clear an obstruction when a brick   12.____
wall is being built, the MOST suitable tool to use is number

    A. 16   B. 19   C. 20   D. 33

13. A large number of wood screws can be screwed into a board MOST quickly by using   13.____
number

    A. 7   B. 8   C. 11   D. 17

14. A number of different diameter holes can be MOST easily bored through a heavy wood   14.____
plank by using number

    A. 3   B. 13   C. 21   D. 31

15. The tool to use in order to form threads in a hole in a steel block is number   15.____

    A. 2   B. 3   C. 27   D. 31

16. Curved designs in thin wood are *preferably* cut with number   16.____

    A. 12   B. 23   C. 29   D. 37

17. The driving of Phillips-head screws requires the use of number   17.____

    A. 7   B. 8   C. 11   D. 34

18. In order to properly flare one end of a piece of copper tubing, the tool to use is number   18.____

    A. 13   B. 25   C. 33   D. 35

19. Tool number 16 is used for   19.____

    A. counterboring   B. cutting concrete
    C. countersinking   D. reaming

20. A tool that can be used to drill a hole in a concrete wall to install a lead anchor is number   20._____

    A. 3   B. 16   C. 21   D. 25

21. After cutting a piece of steel pipe, the burrs are BEST removed from the inside edge with   21._____
number

    A. 6   B. 13   C. 16   D. 33

22. The MOST convenient tool for measuring the depth of a 1/2-inch diameter hole is num-   22._____
ber

    A. 24   B. 31   C. 32   D. 36

23. A 1" x 1" x 1/8" angle iron would *usually* be cut using number   23._____

    A. 12   B. 26   C. 29   D. 37

24. Wood screws located in positions NOT accessible to an ordinary screwdriver would be   24._____
removed using number

    A. 2   B. 8   C. 13   D. 30

25. A small hole can be quickly bored through a 1/8-inch thick plywood board with number   25._____

    A. 3   B. 7   C. 21   D. 31

KEY (CORRECT ANSWERS)

1.	A	11.	B
2.	A	12.	B
3.	B	13.	A
4.	A	14.	D
5.	B	15.	B
6.	C	16.	B
7.	A	17.	D
8.	A	18.	D
9.	A	19.	C
10.	C	20.	D

21.	D
22.	A
23.	D
24.	B
25.	C

EXAMINATION SECTION
TEST 1

DIRECTIONS: Each question or incomplete statement is followed by several suggested answers or completions. Select the one that BEST answers the question or completes the statement. *PRINT THE LETTER OF THE CORRECT ANSWER IN THE SPACE AT THE RIGHT.*

1. Reinforced concrete is concrete which has been strengthened by the addition of   1.____

    A. long steel reinforcing rods
    B. chemical strengtheners
    C. additional cement
    D. additional coarse aggregate

2. An employee will *most likely* avoid accidental injury if he   2.____

    A. stops to rest frequently   B. works alone
    C. keeps mentally alert   D. works very slowly

3. To close off one opening in a pipe tee when the line connecting into it is to be temporarily removed, it is necessary to use a   3.____

    A. pipe cap   B. pipe plug   C. nipple   D. bushing

4. A 1-inch pipe is to span exactly 12 inches between the faces of two fittings. If a pipe thread table shows that 1- inch pipe has good threads extending for a distance of 11/16 inch at each end, then the necessary piece of 1- inch pipe must be cut to a total length of   4.____

    A. 12 11/32"   B. 12 11/16"   C. 13 1/32"   D. 13 3/8"

5. The tool that should be used to cut a 1" x 4" plank down to a 3" width is a   5.____

    A. hacksaw   B. crosscut saw
    C. rip saw   D. backsaw

6. A newly appointed helper would be expected to do his work in the manner prescribed by his foreman because   6.____

    A. it insures discipline
    B. no other method would work
    C. good results are more certain with less supervision
    D. it permits speed-up

7. Employees using supplies from one of the first-aid kits available throughout the subway are required to submit an immediate report of the occurrence. Logical reasoning shows that the MOST important reason for this report is so that the   7.____

    A. supplies used will be sure to be replaced
    B. first-aid kit can be properly sealed again
    C. employee will be credited for his action
    D. record of first-aid supplies will be up to date

8. The BEST immediate first-aid treatment for a scraped knee is to   8.____

   A. apply plain vase line   B. use a knee splint
   C. apply heat   D. wash it with soap and water

9. Two identical, small steel beams are, respectively, 32 feet and 26 feet long. The LEAST   9.____
   load can be supported by a chain hoist that is hung

   A. near one end of the shorter beam
   B. at the mid-point of the longer beam
   C. near one end of the longer beam
   D. at the mid-point of the shorter beam

10. If the drawing of a carpentry detail is made to a scale of 3/4" to the foot, a scaled mea-   10.____
    surement of 6" would represent a length of

    A. 3/8 inches   B. 8 inches   C. 4 1/2 feet   D. 8 feet

11. If, when you are using an extension light with a long cord, the light should go out sud-   11.____
    denly, the FIRST thing you should do is to

    A. inspect the cord for a broken wire
    B. replace the bulb with a new one
    C. check the fuses in the supply circuit
    D. check if the plug is still in the outlet

12. The MOST important reason for covering a wood door with sheet metal is to make the   12.____
    door more

    A. burglar-proof
    B. fire-resistant
    C. termite-proof
    D. resistant to natural decay and deterioration

13. It is customary to stiffen long wood floor joists by the use of   13.____

    A. bridging   B. shoring   C. headers   D. boxing

14. When carrying pipe, employees are cautioned against lifting with the fingers inserted in   14.____
    the ends. The *probable* reason for this caution is to avoid the possibility of

    A. dropping and damaging pipe
    B. getting dirt and perspiration on inside of pipe
    C. cutting the fingers on edge of pipe
    D. straining finger muscles

15. The circumference of a circle is given by the formula, $C = \pi D$, where C is the circumfer-   15.____
    ence, D is the diameter and π is about 3 1/7. If a coil of 20 turns of steel cable has an
    average diameter of 16 inches, the TOTAL length of cable on the coil is NEAREST to
    _____ feet.

    A. 45   B. 65   C. 75   D. 85

16. Threads are cut on the ends of a length of steel pipe by the use of a 16.____

    A. brace and bit   B. counterbore
    C. stock and die   D. doweling jig

17. If you have been fairly proficient in most tasks which have been assigned to you, but then run into considerable difficulty in properly operating some new equipment, it would be MOST logical to assume that 17.____

    A. you have not been properly instructed in its operation
    B. this new equipment is too complicated for the average helper
    C. you are not capable of mastering this equipment
    D. you prefer manual methods to mechanical ones

18. The MOST valid reason for a particular job having a time limit set on it is that 18.____

    A. maximum output can only be secured in this way
    B. this particular job is urgent
    C. the men will be kept continuously busy
    D. the best quality of work is thus achieved

19. Artificial respiration after a severe electric shock is ALWAYS necessary when the shock results in 19.____

    A. unconsciousness   B. stoppage of breathing
    C. bleeding   D. a burn

20. A newly appointed employee is sometimes made the object of practical jokes by some thoughtless people in his gang. The *proper* way for him to handle such a situation would be to 20.____

    A. refer such incidents to his foreman
    B. warn the entire gang that all such jokes at his expense must stop at once
    C. play a few practical jokes on the other men himself
    D. ignore such incidents and they will stop

21. Galvanized sheet metal is coated with 21.____

    A. zinc   B. lead   C. tin   D. copper

22. The MOST common cause for a workman to lose his balance and fall when working from an extension ladder is 22.____

    A. too much spring in the ladder
    B. sideways sliding of the top
    C. exerting a heavy pull on an object which gives suddenly
    D. working on something directly behind the ladder

23. The process of making fresh concrete watertight, durable and strong after it has been poured is called 23.____

    A. air-entraining   B. finishing
    C. curing   D. accelerating

24. The distance Y between adjacent edges of the evenly spaced 3/4" diameter holes in the plate is   24.____

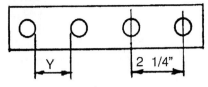

 A. 3/4"   B. 15/16"   C. 1 1/2"   D. 1 7/8"

25. The area of the shaded portion of the circle shown is found by multiplying one-fourth of the square of the diameter, D, by 22/7 and by   25.____

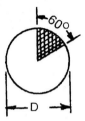

 A. 1/8   B. 1/6   C. 1/4   D. 1/3

KEY (CORRECT ANSWERS)

1.	A		11.	D
2.	C		12.	B
3.	B		13.	A
4.	D		14.	C
5.	C		15.	D
6.	C		16.	C
7.	A		17.	A
8.	D		18.	B
9.	B		19.	B
10.	D		20.	A

21.	A
22.	C
23.	C
24.	C
25.	B

TEST 2

DIRECTIONS: Each question or incomplete statement is followed by several suggested answers or completions. Select the one that BEST answers the question or completes the Statement. *PRINT THE LETTER OF THE CORRECT ANSWER IN THE SPACE AT THE RIGHT.*

1.   It is NOT necessary to wear protective goggles when

   A.   drilling rivet holes in a steel beam
   B.   sharpening tools on a power grinder
   C.   welding a steel plate to a pipe column
   D.   laying up a cinder block partition

1._____

2.   Hollow tile masonry units are provided with their characteristic cells or voids in order to

   A.   allow for packing with greater quantities of mortar
   B.   provide paths for better wall drainage
   C.   provide space for piping to run through
   D.   achieve reduction in the weight of the units

2._____

3.   After rivets have been driven, they are *usually* struck with a light hammer to

   A.   improve the shape of the rivet heads
   B.   give the rivets a tighter fit
   C.   give the rivet heads the necessary caulking
   D.   detect any loose rivets

3._____

4.   An order of 600 feet of 1-inch pipe is shipped in 24-foot lengths. The number of 7-foot pieces that can be cut from this shipment is

   A.   25   B.   72   C.   75   D.   85

4._____

5.   A bit brace can be locked so that the bit will turn in only one direction by means of a

   A.   feed screw   B.   rachet device
   C.   universal chuck   D.   ball-bearing device

5._____

6.   A helper should NOT make suggestions for new job procedures

   A.   because he cannot compete with the more experienced employees
   B.   unless he has given some thought to the matter
   C.   because he is not paid for such work
   D.   unless he first receives assurance he will receive credit

6._____

7.   The transit authority gives some of its maintenance employees instruction in first aid. The *most likely* reason for doing this is to

   A.   eliminate the need for calling a doctor in case of accident
   B.   reduce the number of accidents
   C.   lower the cost of accidents to the Transit Authority
   D.   provide temporary emergency treatment in case of accident

7._____

8. The BEST immediate first aid if a chemical solution splashes into the eyes is to

    A. protect the eyes from the light by bandaging
    B. flush the eyes with large quantities of clean water
    C. cause tears to flow by staring at a bright light
    D. rub the eyes dry with a towel

8.____

9. It is important to make certain that a ladle does NOT contain water before using it to scoop up molten solder, since the water may

    A. cause serious personal injury
    B. prevent the solder from sticking
    C. cool the solder
    D. dilute the solder

9.____

10. The sewer gas and other foul air in a plumbing system is prevented from passing into the room containing a plumbing fixture by means of a device called a

    A. trap   B. vent   C. siphon   D. riser

10.____

11. On your first day on the job as a helper, you are assigned to work with a maintainer. During the course of the work, you realize that the maintainer is about to violate a basic safety rule. In this case, the BEST thing for you to do is to

    A. immediately call it to his attention
    B. say nothing until he actually violates the rule and then call it to his attention
    C. say nothing, but later report this action to the foreman
    D. walk away from him so that you will not become involved

11.____

12. In order to clear the jamb, the lock-edge of a door must be beveled. The bevel must be GREATEST when the door is

    A. wide and thin   B. wide and thick
    C. narrow and thin   D. narrow and thick

12.____

13. A new 9" thick concrete floor is to be poured in a 90' x 100' cellar. This will require a quantity of concrete of about _____ cubic yards.

    A. 47   B. 562   C. 250   D. 6750

13.____

14. A reamer is used to

    A. enlarge drilled holes to an exact size
    B. punch holes to desired size
    C. line up adjacent holes
    D. lay out holes before drilling

14.____

15. You will *probably* be MOST highly regarded by your superiors if you show that

    A. you like your work by asking all the questions you can about it
    B. you are on the job by volunteering information whenever you think someone has violated a rule
    C. you are interested in improving the job by continually offering suggestions
    D. you are willing to do your share by completing assigned tasks properly and on time

15.____

16. Telephones are located alongside of the subway tracks for emergency use. The locations of these telephones are indicated by blue lights. The reason for selecting this color rather than green is that

    A. a blue light can be seen for greater distance
    B. blue lights are easier to buy
    C. green cannot be seen by a person who is color-blind
    D. green lights are used for train signals

16.____

17. If you had to telephone for an ambulance because of an accident, the MOST important information for you to give the person who answered the telephone would be the

    A. exact time of the accident
    B. place where the ambulance is needed
    C. cause of the accident
    D. names and addresses of those injured

17.____

18. The height of a station platform above the running rails is closest to

    A. 6 inches   B. 1 foot   C. 4 feet   D. 8 feet

18.____

19. The average number of steps in a flight of stairs in the subway between a station platform and the mezzanine above is *approximately*

    A. 5 to 10   B. 15 to 20   C. 25 to 30   D. 35 to 40

19.____

20. MOST handrails on subway stairs are made of

    A. steel   B. wood
    C. plastic   D. wrought iron

20.____

21. MOST steel columns in the subway are

    A. unpainted   B. painted
    C. concrete covered   D. tile covered

21.____

22. The tool shown at the right is a
    A. countersink
    B. counterbore
    C. star drill
    D. burring reamer

22.____

23. The saw shown at the right would be used to cut
    A. curved designs in thin wood
    B. strap iron
    C. asphalt tiles to fit against walls
    D. soft lead pipe

23.____

24. The tool shown at the right is a
    A. float
    B. finishing trowel
    C. hawk
    D. roofing seamer

24.____

25. The hammer shown to the right would be used by a
    A. carpenter
    B. bricklayer
    C. tinsmith
    D. plumber

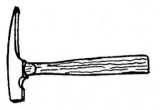

25.____

_____

KEY (CORRECT ANSWERS)

1.	D		11.	A
2.	D		12.	D
3.	A		13.	C
4.	C		14.	A
5.	B		15.	D
6.	B		16.	D
7.	D		17.	B
8.	B		18.	C
9.	A		19.	B
10.	A		20.	B

21. B
22. D
23. A
24. A
25. B

_____

TEST 3

DIRECTIONS: Each question or incomplete statement is followed by several suggested answers or completions. Select the one that BEST answers the question or completes the statement. *PRINT THE LETTER OF THE CORRECT ANSWER IN THE SPACE AT THE RIGHT.*

QUESTIONS 1-8.

Questions 1 to 8 are based on the sketch below representing the floor plan of a one-story frame structure. Consult this drawing when answering these questions.

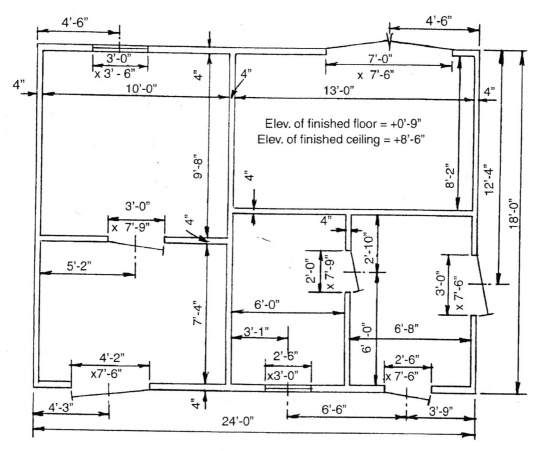

1. The number of windows shown is   1.____

    A. 2   B. 4   C. 6   D. 8

2. The number of exterior door openings shown is   2.____

    A. 2   B. 4   C. 6   D. 8

3. The dimensions of the SMALLEST door opening are   3.____

    A. 2'-6" x 3'-0"   B. 2'-0" x 7'-6"   C. 2'-0" x 7'-9"   D. 2'-6" x 7'-6"

4. There is NO room which has dimensions of   4.____

    A. 7'-4" x 10'-0"   B. 6'-0" x 8'-10"   C. 6'-8" x 8'-2"   D. 6'-8" x 8'-10"

5. The height of the rooms is   5.___

    A. 7'-6"   B. 7'-9"   C. 8'-6"   D. 9'-3"

6. The net floor area, in square feet, of the only corner room NOT provided with an exterior   6.
    door is about

    A. 53   B. 73   C. 97   D. 106

7. The total outside perimeter, in feet, of the structure is   7.___

    A. 18   B. 24   C. 42   D. 84

8. The total number of inside partitions is   8.___

    A. 4   B. 5   C. 6   D. 7

9. If you and another helper are assigned to a hard and tedious job and your co-worker is   9.___
    not doing a reasonable share of the work, your BEST procedure is to

    A. slow down to his rate
    B. try to persuade him to do his share
    C. do your share and quit
    D. stop and register a complaint with the foreman before continuing

10. A transit employee is required to make a written report of any unusual occurrence   10.___
    promptly. The BEST reason for requiring such promptness is that

    A. it helps prevent similar occurrences
    B. the employee is less likely to forget details
    C. there is always a tendency to do a better job under pressure
    D. the report may be too long if made at an employee's convenience

11. There are a few workers who are seemingly prone to accidents and who, regardless of   11.___
    their assigned job, have a higher accident rate than the average worker. If your co-worker
    is known to be such an individual, the BEST course for you to pursue would be to

    A. do most of the assigned work yourself
    B. refuse to work with this individual
    C. provide him with a copy of all rules and regulations
    D. personally check all safety precautions on each job

12. When a piece of rough timber is dressed on all four sides, the width and thickness of the   12.___
    dressed piece will be LESS than the original width and thickness of the rough piece by

    A. 1/16" or 1/8"   B. 1/8" or 1/4"
    C. 3/8" or 1/2"   D. 5/8" or 3/4"

13. If a helper finds two orders on his headquarters bulletin board giving conflicting instruc-   13.___
    tions with regard to his work, his MOST helpful action would be to

    A. call it to the attention of his superior
    B. comply with the order which is easier to follow
    C. follow the order which is best in his judgment
    D. defer that part of the work until a clarifying order is posted

14. When sheet metal is riveted, a specified minimum distance must be provided between the edge of the sheet and the nearest rivet in order to prevent

    A. the rivet head from working loose
    B. the rivet from being sheared
    C. tearing of the sheet between the edge of the rivet hole and the edge of the sheet
    D. excessive stress concentrations on the rivet

14.____

15. If the maintainer to whom you are assigned gives you a job to be done in a certain way and, after starting the job, you think of another method which you are convinced is better, you should

    A. follow the procedure given by the maintainer since he most likely would insist on his method anyway
    B. try your own method since the maintainer probably will not know the difference
    C. tell the foreman about your method the next time he appears at your job
    D. request the maintainer's opinion of your method before proceeding further

15.____

16. Concrete (a mixture of cement, sand and coarse aggregate, with added water), if made from 1 part of one material 2 parts of a second material and 4 parts of the remaining material, is known as 1:2:4 concrete. It would be LOGICAL to conclude that the parts would be

    A. 1 cement, 2 coarse aggregate, 4 sand
    B. 1 coarse aggregate, 2 cement, 4 sand
    C. 1 sand, 2 coarse aggregate, 4 cement
    D. 1 cement, 2 sand, 4 coarse aggregate

16.____

17. You are assigned to determine the *approximate* total number of bricks in a large closely stacked rectangular pile. The MOST practical method for doing this is to

    A. multiply the three dimensions of the pile in feet and divide by the cubic feet in one brick
    B. count all the bricks individually in the face of the pile and multiply by the number of bricks in the width
    C. count the number of bricks in approximately one-quarter of the pile and multiply by four
    D. weigh the bricks and divide by the weight of one brick

17.____

18. A vertical wood framing member used in making a wall for a building is called a

    A. joist   B. beam   C. stud   D. header

18.____

19. Good practice requires that the end of a piece of water pipe be reamed to remove the inside burr after it has been cut to length to

    A. finish the pipe accurately to length
    B. make the threading easier
    C. avoid the cutting of the worker's hands
    D. allow free passage for the flow of water

19.____

20. The eight 2-foot high cartons and the six 4-foot high cartons shown are stacked in two separate rows, each row being one carton high. If these fourteen cartons are to be arranged into 5 piles of equal height, the MAXIMUM number of different arrangements by which this can be achieved is

20.____

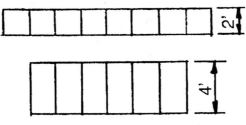

   A. 1   B. 2   C. 3   D. 4

21. When the 100 lb. weight is being slowly hoisted up by the pulley shown below, the downward pull on the ceiling to which the pulley is attached is _____ lbs.

21.____

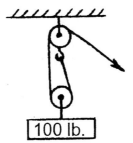

   A. 50   B. 100   C. 150   D. 200

22. In order to rearrange the bricks shown into the FEWEST equal piles, the number of bricks required to be moved is

22.____

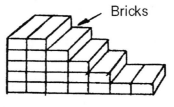

Bricks

   A. 2   B. 4   C. 7   D. 11

23. Shown below is a semicircular metal sheet with diameter 1-2. The LARGEST right-triangular piece can be cut from this semicircle when the base of the triangle is the diameter 1-2 and the apex of the triangle is at point

23.___

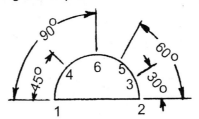

   A. 3   B. 4   C. 5   D. 6

24. In making up the piping shown, one piece of pipe was cut the wrong length so that the union at location "A" would not meet as shown. The pipe which was cut wrong MUST have been pipe number

24.____

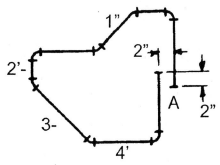

   A. 1   B. 2   C. 3   D. 4

25. The flat cut sheet, with cut-outs as shown, can be bent along the dotted lines to makes one of the shapes shown. The resulting shape is No.

25.____

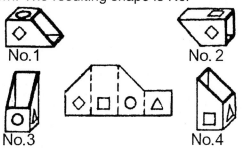

   A. 1   B. 2   C. 3   D. 4

KEY (CORRECT ANSWERS)

1.	A		11.	D
2.	B		12.	C
3.	C		13.	A
4.	C		14.	C
5.	B		15.	D
6.	C		16.	D
7.	D		17.	A
8.	A		18.	C
9.	B		19.	D
10.	B		20.	C

21.	C
22.	C
23.	D
24.	C
25.	B

———

TEST 4

DIRECTIONS: Each question or incomplete statement is followed by several suggested answers or completions. Select the one that BEST answers the question or completes the statement. *PRINT THE LETTER OF THE CORRECT ANSWER IN THE SPACE AT THE RIGHT.*

1. When using a brace and bit to bore a hole completely through a partition, it is MOST important to

   A. lean heavily on the brace and bit
   B. maintain a steady turning speed all through the job
   C. have the body in a position that will not be easily thrown off balance
   D. reverse the direction of the bit at frequent intervals

   1.____

2. Flux is used when soldering two pieces of sheet metal together in order to

   A. conduct the heat of the soldering iron to the sheets
   B. lower the melting point of the solder
   C. glue the solder to the sheets
   D. protect the sheet metal from oxidizing when heated by the soldering iron

   2.____

3. If you are holding a heavy load by the pull rope on a block and tackle, your BEST procedure is to

   A. take a snub around a fixed object
   B. tie the rope around your waist
   C. stand on the rope and hold the end
   D. pull sideways to jam the rope in the block

   3.____

4. To measure the width of a piece of finish flooring, include

   A. the groove but not the tongue
   B. the tongue but not the groove
   C. neither the tongue nor the groove
   D. both the tongue and the groove

   4.____

5. A board 10'-6" long is to have 5 holes drilled along its length. The distances between centers of adjacent holes are to be equal and the distance from each end of the board to the center of the nearest hole is to be twice the distance between centers of adjacent holes. The distance between centers of adjacent holes will be

   A. 14"   B. 15 3/4"   C. 18"   D. 21"

   5.____

6. If a steel square is not available, a rectangular wood form for concrete can be squared up by the use of a

   A. steel tape   B. set of trammel points
   C. shooting board   D. level

   6.____

7. If you are assigned by your foreman to a job which you do not understand, you should

   A. explain this and request further instructions from your foreman
   B. try to do the job because you learn from experience
   C. do the job to the best of your ability as that is all that can be expected
   D. ask a more experienced helper how to proceed with the Job

   7.____

8. A rule of the transit system states that, "In walking on the track, walk opposite the direction of traffic on that track if possible." By logical reasoning, the *principle* safety idea behind this rule is that the man on the track

    A. is more likely to see an approaching train
    B. will be seen more readily by the motorman
    C. need not be as careful
    D. is better able to judge the speed of the train

8.____

9. If a person has a deep puncture in his finger caused by a sharp nail, the BEST immediate first-aid procedure would be to

    A. prevent air from reaching the wound
    B. stop all bleeding
    C. encourage bleeding by exerting pressure aroung the injured area
    D. probe the wound for steel particles

9.____

10. An outstanding cause of accidents is the improper use of tools.
The MOST helpful conclusion you can draw from this statement is that

    A. most tools are defective
    B. many accidents involving the use of tools occur because of poor working habits
    C. most workers are poorly trained
    D. many accidents involving the use of tools are unavoidable

10.____

11. If it is necessary to shorten the length of a bolt by cutting through the threaded portion, the SIMPLEST procedure to avoid difficulty with the thread is to

    A. cut parallel to the threads in the groove of the thread
    B. run on a die after cutting
    C. turn on a nut past the cutting point prior to cutting
    D. clear the injured thread with a 3-cornered file

11.____

12. If concrete which is being put into a sloping metal chute for deposit into place has difficulty flowing down the chute, the BEST remedy would be to

    A. pound the chute with a sledge hammer
    B. add more water to the concrete mix
    C. increase the slope of the chute if possible
    D. oil the chute to reduce friction

12.____

13. When a window in a building under construction has been glazed, it is *usually* marked with a white X across the glass to

    A. call attention to the fact that the window is no longer open
    B. remind the clean-up gang to wash this window
    C. mark the progress of the glazing work in the building
    D. help reduce vandalism

13.____

14. A wood crate with a lid is 3 feet wide, 4 feet long and 5 feet deep, and is to be covered with plywood. If 1/4" strips 4" wide, are used for this job, the number of linear feet of these strips that will be required is *most nearly*

    A. 31   B. 60   C. 94   D. 282

14.__

15. The square slot cut in the piece shown is *most nearly*   15.____

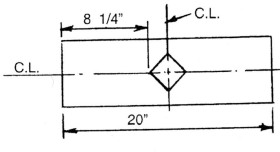

   A. 2" x 2"   B. 2 1/2" x 2 1/2"
   C. 3" X 3"   D. 3 1/2" x 3 1/2"

16. After the cross-hatched right-triangular area has been removed, the large right-triangular   16.____
    piece shown will have a remaining area of only _____ square inches.

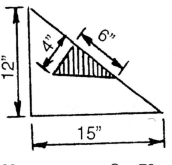

   A. 24   B. 66   C. 78   D. 90

17. If it is necessary to lift up and hold one heavy part of a piece of equipment with a pinch   17.____
    bar so that there is enough clearance to work with the hands under the part, one IMPOR-
    TANT precaution is to

   A. wear gloves
   B. watch the bar to be ready if it slips
   C. work as fast as possible
   D. insert a temporary block to hold the part

18. The structural member that is MOST commonly used as a lintel in buildings with a struc-   18.____
    tural steel framework is the

   A. angle   B. channel   C. plate   D. zee-bar

19. Practically all valves used in plumbing work are made so that the handwheel is turned   19.____
    clockwise instead of counterclockwise to close the valve. The *probable* reason is that

   A. it is easier to remember since screws and nuts move inward when turned clock-
       wise
   B. the hand wheel is less likely to loosen
   C. greater force can be exerted
   D. most people are right-handed

20. Brickwork is said to be laid up in common bond when it 20.____

    A.   has a header course after every five stretcher courses
    B.   is made up entirely of header courses
    C.   is made up entirely of stretcher courses
    D.   has a stretcher course after every five header courses

21. Sharpening a hand saw consists of 21.____

    A.   jointing, shaping, setting and filing
    B.   adzing, clinching, forging and machining
    C.   brazing, chiseling, grinding and mitering
    D.   bushing, dressing, lapping and machining

22. When you are newly assigned as a helper to an experienced maintainer, he is *most likely* 22.____
to give you good training if your attitude is that

    A.   he should do the job where little is to be learned
    B.   he is responsible for your progress
    C.   you have the basic knowledge but lack the details
    D.   you need the benefit of his experience

23. The book of rules and regulations states that employees must give notice in person or by 23.____
telephone of their intention to be absent from work at least one hour before they are
scheduled to report for duty. The MOST logical reason for having this rule is that

    A.   it allows time to check the employee's excuse
    B.   it has a nuisance value in limiting absences
    C.   the employee's time record can be corrected in advance
    D.   a substitute can be provided

24. The MOST important reason for insisting on neatness in maintenance quarters is that it 24.____

    A.   increases the available storage space
    B.   makes for good employee morale
    C.   prevents tools from becoming rusty
    D.   decreases the chances of accidents to employees

25. There are many steel ladders and stairways installed in the subway for the use of transit 25.____
workers. Their GREATEST danger is that they

    A.   have sharp edges causing cuts
    B.   are slippery when greasy and wet
    C.   cause colds
    D.   have no "give" and thus cause fatigue

KEY (CORRECT ANSWERS)

1.	C		11.	C
2.	D		12.	C
3.	A		13.	A
4.	A		14.	D
5.	B		15.	B
6.	A		16.	C
7.	A		17.	D
8.	A		18.	A
9.	C		19.	A
10.	B		20.	A

21.	A
22.	D
23.	D
24.	D
25.	B

———

EXAMINATION SECTION
TEST 1

DIRECTIONS: Each question or incomplete statement is followed by several suggested answers or completions. Select the one that BEST answers the question or completes the statement. *PRINT THE LETTER OF THE CORRECT ANSWER IN THE SPACE AT THE RIGHT.*

Questions 1-8.

DIRECTIONS: Questions 1 through 8, inclusive, are based on the paragraph *JACKS* shown below. When answering these questions, refer to this paragraph.

JACKS

When using a jack, a workman should cheek the capacity plate or other markings on the jack to make sure the device is heavy enough to support the load. Where there is no plate, capacity should be determined and painted on the side of the jack. The workman should see that jacks are well lubricated, but only at points where lubrication is specified, and should inspect them for broken teeth or faulty holding fixtures. A jack should never be thrown or dropped upon the floors such treatment may crack or distort the metal, thus causing the jack to break when a load is lifted. It is important that the floor or ground surface upon which the jack is placed be level and clean, and the safe limit of floor loading is not exceeded. If the surface is earth, the jack base should be set on heavy wood blocking, preferably hardwood, of sufficient size that the blocking will not turn over, shift, or sink. If the surface is not perfectly level, the jack may be set on blocking, which should be leveled by wedges securely placed so that they cannot be brushed or forced out of place. "Extenders" of wood or metal, intended to provide a higher rise where a jack cannot reach up to load or lift it high enough, should never be used. Instead, a larger jack should be obtained or higher blocking which is correspond-ingly wider and longer — should be placed under the jack. All lifts should be vertical with the jack correctly centered for the lift. The base of the jack should be on a perfectly level surface, and the jack head, with its hardwood shim, should bear against a perfectly level meeting sur-face.

1.   To make sure the jack is heavy enough to support a certain load, the workman should   1._____

    A.   lubricate the jack
    B.   shim the jack
    C.   check the capacity plate
    D.   use a long handle

2.   A jack should be lubricated   2._____

    A.   after using   B.   before painting
    C.   only at specified points   D.   to prevent slipping

3.   The workman should inspect a jack for   3._____

    A.   manufacturer's name   B.   broken teeth
    C.   paint peeling   D.   broken wedges

4. Metal parts on a jack may crack if   4.____

    A. the jack is thrown on the floor
    B. the load is leveled
    C. blocking is used
    D. the handle is too short

5. It would NOT be a safe practice for a workman to   5.____

    A. center the jack under the load
    B. set the jack on a level surface
    C. use hardwood for blocking
    D. use *extenders* to reach up to the load

6. Wedges may safely be used to   6.____

    A. replace a broken tooth
    B. prevent the overloading of a jack
    C. level the blocking under a jack
    D. straighten distorted metal

7. Blocking should be   7.____

    A. made of a soft wood
    B. placed between the jack base and the earth surface
    C. well lubricated
    D. used to repair a broken tooth

8. A hardwood shim should be used   8.____

    A. between the head and its meeting surface
    B. under the jack
    C. as a filler
    D. to level a surface

9. When a long pipe is being carried, the front end should be held high and the rear end   9.____
low.
The MAIN reason for this is to

    A. prevent injury to others when turning blind corners
    B. make it easier to carry
    C. prevent injury to the man carrying the pipe
    D. prevent damage to the pipe

10. As a serviceman, you notice a condition in the shop which you believe to be dangerous,   10.____
but is under the jurisdiction of another department.
You should

    A. immediately notify your superior
    B. call the assistant general superintendent
    C. take no action, as your department is not involved
    D. send a letter to the department involved

11. All employees should regularly read the bulletin board at their job location MAINLY in order to

    A. learn what previously posted material has been removed
    B. show that they have an interest in the department
    C. see whether other employees have something for sale
    D. become familiar with new orders or procedures posted on it

11._____

12. The book of rules and regulations states that employees must give notice, in person or by telephone, at least one hour before they are scheduled to report for duty, of their intention to be absent from work.
The LOGICAL reason for having this rule is that

    A. the employees' time can be recorded in advance
    B. a substitute can be provided
    C. it allows time to check the employees' record
    D. it reduces absenteeism

12._____

13. When tools are found in poor condition, the reason is MOST often because of

    A. misuse of tools
    B. their use by more than one person
    C. defects in the manufacture of tools
    D. their use in construction work

13._____

14. When lifting a heavy object, a man should NOT

    A. twist his body while lifting
    B. bend knees
    C. have secure footing
    D. take a firm grip on the object

14._____

15. The MAIN purpose of the periodic inspection of machines and equipment is to

    A. locate stolen property
    B. make the workmen more familiar with the equipment
    C. discover minor faults before they develop into more serious conditions
    D. encourage the workmen to take better care of their equipment

15._____

16. If a serviceman does not understand a verbal order given him by his foreman, he should

    A. do the best he can
    B. ask for a different assignment
    C. ask the foreman to explain it
    D. look it up in the book of rules

16._____

17. A rule prohibits indulgence in intoxicating liquor, or being under its influence, while on duty. This rule is rigidly enforced in order to

    A. prevent an employee from endangering himself or others
    B. help reduce littering
    C. eliminate absenteeism
    D. help promote temperance

17._____

18. As a newly appointed serviceman, your foreman would expect you to 18.____

    A. make many blunders
    B. repair car equipment
    C. study car maintenance on your own time
    D. follow his instructions closely

19. Your work will probably be MOST appreciated by your superior if you 19.____

    A. continually ask questions about your work
    B. keep him informed whenever you think someone has violated a rule
    C. continually come to him with suggestions for improving the job
    D. do your share by completing assigned tasks properly and on time

20. One of your fellow workers has to leave work a half-hour early and asks you to punch his 20.____
time card for him.
You should

    A. punch out for him, but be sure to tell your supervisor
    B. tell him that no one is allowed to punch out someone else's time card
    C. punch out for him because you know he would do the same for you
    D. tell him he must promise to stay an extra half-hour tomorrow before you punch out
       for him

21. As far as is practicable, fiber rope should not be allowed to become wet, as this hastens 21.____
decay. The MOST logical conclusion to be drawn from this statement is that

    A. fiber rope is stronger than nylon rope
    B. shrinkage of wet rope is not a problem
    C. nylon rope is better than wire rope
    D. wet rope should be thoroughly dried before being stored away

22. The MAIN reason that gear cases are stacked on a pallet is to 22.____

    A. help servicemen find gear cases quickly
    B. help stockmen keep track of gear cases
    C. avoid hand-carrying of gear cases
    D. prevent damage to gear cases

23. If you are holding a heavy load by the pull rope on a block and tackle, your BEST proce- 23.____
dure is to

    A. let the rope hang loose
    B. snub the rope around a fixed object
    C. pull sideways to jam the rope in the block
    D. stand on the rope and hold the end

24. Modern electric power tools such as electric drills come with a third conductor in the 24.____
power cord, which is used to connect the case of the tool to a grounded part of the electric outlet.
The reason for this additional electrical conductor is to

A. protect the user of the tool should the motor short out to the case
B. provide for continued operation of the tool should the regular grounded line-wire open
C. eliminate sparking between the tool and the material being worked upon
D. provide a spare wire for additional controls

25. When a long ladder is being used, a length of rope should be tied from its lowest rung to a fixed support in order to prevent   25._____

A. breaking the rungs
B. the ladder from slipping
C. anyone from removing the ladder
D. anyone from walking under the ladder

26. When the level of the liquid in a storage battery on a Hi-lo truck is too low, the proper liquid to add to bring the level up to normal is   26._____

A. salt   B. alkaline solution
C. acid solution   D. distilled water

27. The MOST important reason for servicemen to keep their work areas neat and clean is that it   27._____

A. makes more room for storage
B. makes for happier workers
C. prevents tools from being broken
D. decreases the chances of accidents to workmen

28. The one of the following which is the BEST example of a material that does NOT burn easily is   28._____

A. canvas   B. paper   C. wood   D. asbestos

29. The CHIEF reason for not letting oily rags or dust cloths accumulate in storage closets is that they   29._____

A. look dirty
B. may start a fire by spontaneous combustion
C. take up space which may be used for more important purposes
D. may drip oil onto the floor

30. The MOST logical reason for a serviceman to blow out electrical and mechanical equipment under car bodies before they are worked on by maintainers is to   30._____

A. cool the equipment for the maintainers
B. prevent rusting of equipment and parts
C. prevent the maintainers from getting dirty while working
D. prevent fires caused by heavy accumulation of dust

31. The liquid in heavy duty hydraulic jacks used in the car shops is   31._____

A. water   B. oil   C. mercury   D. alcohol

32. It is not considered good practice to paint portable wooden ladders.   32.____
The MOST logical reason for this is that the paint

    A. would quickly wear off
    B. might hide serious defects
    C. might rub off on a supporting wall
    D. would dry out the rungs

33. In order to lift a loaded pallet overhead by means of a crane, it would be MOST desirable   33.____
to use a

    A. single wire rope sling   B. long crowbar
    C. pallet sling   D. rope splice

34. Of the following methods, the one which is the BEST way to keep rust off metal tools is to   34.____

    A. keep them dry and oil them once in a while
    B. air blast them
    C. file or grind them often
    D. wash them carefully with warm water

35. A Hi-Lo truck delivering a compressor to a work area approaches a closed door.   35.____
The proper procedure for the Hi-Lo operator to follow is to

    A. open the door while standing on the operating end of the Hi-Lo truck
    B. open the door with the platform of the Hi-Lo truck
    C. stop the Hi-Lo truck, wedge open the door, and then proceed
    D. make a detour and follow a different path

36. The path between the two yellow lines on a main shop floor is used for   36.____

    A. picking up and discharging workers that want a ride on a Hi-Lo
    B. parking area for forklifts
    C. the traffic path for Hi-Lo's and forklifts
    D. storage of materials unloaded from Hi-Lo's

37. While on the way to a storeroom, you notice that oil has dripped on the floor from a jour-   37.____
nal box and created a slipping hazard.
You should

    A. ignore it as it is not your doing
    B. get some *speedi-dry* nearby and spread it over the oil
    C. wait until you return from the storeroom to take care of it
    D. call the supervisor and tell him about it

38. An employee always obeys the safety rules of his department because it has become a   38.____
habit to work by these rules. This is

    A. *good;* such a habit will get work done safely
    B. *bad;* it is hard to change a habit
    C. *good;* safety rules won't work if they have to be thought about
    D. *bad;* safety rules should always be thought about before doing anything and not
         allowed to become a habit

39. If *you* are working in an inspection shop and you notice a trolley bug on one contact shoe of a car, it will mean that 39.____

    A. all contact shoes of the car are *live*
    B. only that contact shoe, that the bug is on, is *live*
    C. only the contact shoes, on the same side of the car that the bug is on, are *live*
    D. only the contact shoes of the one truck are *live*

40. It is necessary for a serviceman to wear a respirator when he is 40.____

    A. climbing a ladder
    B. operating a chipping gun
    C. blowing out the equipment under a car
    D. lubricating gear cases

KEY (CORRECT ANSWERS)

1. C	11. D	21. D	31. B
2. C	12. B	22. C	32. B
3. B	13. A	23. B	33. C
4. A	14. A	24. A	34. A
5. D	15. C	25. B	35. C
6. C	16. C	26. D	36. C
7. B	17. A	27. D	37. B
8. A	18. D	28. D	38. A
9. A	19. D	29. B	39. A
10. A	20. B	30. D	40. C

TEST 2

DIRECTIONS: Each question or incomplete statement is followed by several suggested answers or completions. Select the one that BEST answers the question or completes the statement. *PRINT THE LETTER OF THE CORRECT ANSWER IN THE SPACE AT THE RIGHT.*

1. The type of fire extinguisher which you would NOT use to extinguish a fire around electri- 1.___
   cal circuits is

   A. carbon dioxide   B. dry chemical
   C. water   D. dry sand

2. Artificial respiration is applied when an accident has caused   2.___

   A. breathing difficulties   B. loss of blood
   C. broken ribs   D. burns

3. Workers must NOT wear clothes that are too big when they work near moving machinery   3.___
   because

   A. that kind of dress will attract attention
   B. some part of the clothes can catch in the machinery
   C. big clothes get dirtier
   D. big clothes are hard to replace

4. The MOST likely reason why an employee should make out a report after using the con-   4.___
   tents of a first aid kit is that

   A. he will learn to write a good report
   B. unauthorized use may be prevented
   C. used material will be replaced
   D. a new seal may be provided

5. A shop employee is involved in an accident and severely injures his ankle.   5.___
   If a tourniquet were used, it would be to

   A. keep the ankle warm
   B. prevent infection
   C. prevent the ankle from moving
   D. stop the loss of blood

6. If a serviceman has frequent accidents, it is MOST likely that he is   6.___

   A. a man who works best by himself
   B. satisfied with his job
   C. violating too many safety rules
   D. simply one of those persons who is unlucky

7. In treating a cut finger, the FIRST action should be to   7.___

   A. wash it   B. bandage it
   C. request sick leave   D. apply antiseptic

8. When administering first aid to a person suffering from shock as a result of an accident, it 8.__
   is MOST important to

A. keep him moving
B. prop him up in a sitting position
C. apply artificial respiration
D. cover the person and keep him warm

9. First aid instructions are given to some employees to   9._____

A. eliminate the need for calling a doctor
B. prepare them to give emergency aid
C. collect blood for the blood bank
D. reduce the number of accidents

10. The BEST reason for not using compressed air from an air hose for cleaning dust from   10._____
clothing is that

A. the clothing may be torn by the blast
B. it is a dangerous practice
C. this air contains too much moisture
D. the air pressure will drop too low

11. Protective helmets give servicemen the MOST protection from   11._____

A. falling objects   B. fire
C. eye injuries   D. electric shock

12. Fuses are used in electric circuits   12._____

A. so that electrical power tools cannot short circuit
B. to burn out under an overload before electrical equipment is damaged
C. to increase the amount of current that may be carried in the wires
D. so that workmen can cut off the current without looking for the switch

13. The one of the following that is MOST effective in reducing the danger from hazardous   13._____
vapors is

A. immediate disposal of all wastes
B. labeling all substances clearly
C. maintaining good ventilation
D. wearing proper clothing at all times

14. A serviceman should NEVER look into the arc from an electric welding torch.   14._____
The BEST reason for this is that

A. it can have a harmful effect on his eyes
B. it will distract the welder from his work
C. the serviceman is not allowed to operate a welding torch
D. electric arc welding uses a large electrical current

15. The floors of 2 cars are to be painted with a special test paint. Assume that the floor area   15._____
in each car is 600 square feet. A gallon of this paint will cover 400 square feet.
The number of gallons of this paint that you should pick up at the storeroom to paint
the 2 car floors would be

A. 6   B. 5   C. 4   D. 3

16. Assume that you are sent to the storeroom for 1,000 of 600-volt contact tips which are to be distributed equally to 5 foremen, but you find that the storeroom can only supply you with 825.
If you distribute these 825 tips equally to the 5 foremen, the number of tips that each foreman will receive is

    A. 165   B. 175   C. 190   D. 200

16.____

17. You are asked to fill six 5-gallon cans of oil from a full drum containing 52 gallons. When you have filled the six cans, the number of gallons of oil left in the drun will be MOST NEARLY

    A. 14   B. 16   C. 22   D. 30

17.____

18. A certain wire rope is made up of 6 strands, each strand containing 19 wires.
The total number of wires in this wire rope is

    A. 25   B. 96   C. 114   D. 144

18.____

19. The hook should be the weakest part of any crane, hoist, or sling.
According to this statement, if a particular hook has a rated capacity of 21/2 tons, then the MAXIMUM load thatshould be lifted with this hook is _____ pounds.

    A. 150   B. 3,000   C. 5,000   D. 5,500

19.____

20. Assume that 2 car wheels weigh 635 pounds each and are attached to an axle weighing 1,260 pounds.
The total weight of this assembly is MOST NEARLY _____ pounds.

    A. 1,270   B. 1,520   C. 1,895   D. 2,530

20.____

21. If an employee authorizes his employer to deduct 4% of his $450 weekly salary for a savings bond, the MINIMUM number of weekly deductions required to get enough money to buy a bond costing $54 is

    A. 3   B. 6   C. 8   D. 9

21.___

22. In weighing out a truckful of scrap metal, the scale reads 21,496 lbs. If the empty truck weighs 9,879 lbs., the amount of scrap metal, in pounds, is MOST NEARLY

    A. 10,507   B. 10,602   C. 11,617   D. 12,617

22.____

23. Four trays of material are placed on the body of a delivery truck for delivery to the inspection shop. Each tray is 4 feet wide and 4 feet long.
If these trays are placed side by side on the floor of the delivery truck, together they will cover an area of the floor MOST NEARLY _____ square feet.

    A. 32   B. 48   C. 64   D. 72

23.___

24. Assume that you are operating a degreasing tank and its tray holds 5 gear cases. It takes 40 minutes to clean one tray of gear cases.
At the end of 6 hours of operation (excluding lunch break and loading and unloading time), the number of gear cases cleaned will be

    A. 30   B. 36   C. 45   D. 50

24.___

25. If a serviceman's weekly gross salary is $480, and 20% is deducted for taxes, his take-home pay is

    A. $360   B. $384   C. $420   D. $432

25.____

26. Two-thirds of 10 feet is MOST NEARLY

    A. 6'2"   B. 6'8"   C. 6'11"   D. 7'1"

26.____

27. You are directed to pick up a tray load of brake shoes.
The combined weight of tray and brake shoes is 4,000 pounds. Assume that each brake shoe weighs 40 pounds and the tray weighs 240 pounds.
The number of brake shoes in the tray is MOST NEARLY

    A. 88   B. 94   C. 100   D. 106

27.____

28. The one of the following materials that is used to protect equipment from rain is a

    A. sprinkler   B. tarpaulin
    C. compressor   D. templet

28.____

29. The use of wet rope near power lines and other electrical equipment is

    A. a dangerous practice
    B. sure to interrupt telephone service
    C. recommended as a safe practice
    D. common in the car shop but not in maintenance of way

29.____

Questions 30-34.

DIRECTIONS: Questions 30 through 34, inclusive, are based on thefollowing paragraph, table, and floor plan. Each line in the table contains the name of a certain piece of car equipment together with its destination in the car shop. The floor plan shows a car shop divided into six areas, each with a different code number.

TABLE   CAR SHOP FLOOR PLAN

NAME OF CAR EQUIPMENT	DESTINATION IN CAR SHOP
Journal boxes	Degreasing tanks
Door operators	Car body shop Main
Air compressors	shipping Air brake shop
Unit valves	Truck shop Degreasing
Wheels Gear assemblies	tanks Main shipping
Unit switches Variable load units	Air brake shop
Motor couplings	Degreasing tanks
Motors Brake linkage	Truck shop Degreasing
Fan motors Batteries	tanks Car body shop
Motor generators	Main shipping Car body shop

Overhaul Shop	Air Brake Shop	Main Shipping
AREA 1	AREA 2	AREA 3
Degreasing Tanks	Truck Shop	
AREA 4	AREA 5	
Car Body Shop AREA 6		

In each of Questions 30 through 34, there are the names of four types of car equipment, and a code number for a destination in the car shop. In each question, select the CORRECT combination of equipment name and destination code number as determined by referring to the Table and Car Shop Floor Plan.

30. A. Motor generators: Area 6
     B. Fan motors: Area 5
     C. Motor couplings: Area 1
     D. Motor end housings: Area 2

30._____

31. A. Door operators: Area 3
     B. Air compressors: Area 5
     C. Brake linkage: Area 4
     D. Variable load units: Area 6

31._____

32. A. Batteries: Area 1
     B. Unit switches: Area 3
     C. Motor controllers: Area 2
     D. Fan motors: Area 4

32._____

33. A. Wheels: Area 2
     B. Motor end housings: Area 6
     C. Journal boxes: Area 3
     D. Unit valves: Area 2

33._____

34. A. Gear assemblies: Area 4
     B. Motor couplings: Area 3
     C. Variable load units: Area 6
     D. Unit valves: Area 5

34._____

35. The drawing at the right is an assembly sketch.
     Study the sketch and select the CORRECT assembly
     procedure.
     A. 3 onto 4, 2 onto 5, 1 onto 5, and tighten
     B. 4 onto 3, 1 onto 5, 5 through 4 and 3, tighten 2
         onto 5
     C. 5 into 3, 2 and 1 onto 5, 4 into 3, and tighten
     D. 4 into 3, 5 through 3 and 4, 2 onto 5, 1 onto 5,
         and tighten

35._____

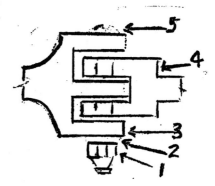

Questions 36-37.

DIRECTIONS: Questions 36 and 37 are based on the following data and sketch. When
              answering these questions, refer to this material.

The average clearance requirements for 2-ton, 3-ton, and 5-ton forklift trucks are shown in the following sketch. Dimensions are: R, the overall length including loads S, the overall widths T, the overall height; U, the minimum permissible width of aisle.

	2-Ton Truck	3-Ton Truck	5-Ton Truck
B	112	118	142
S	45	46	47
T	85	85	85
U	76	79	92

All dimensions are in inches.

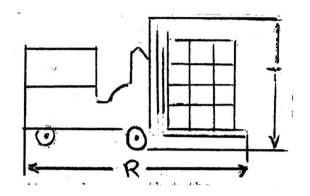

36. From the data given above, it can be seen that the overall length, including load, of a 3-ton truck is _____ inches.

    A. 85   B. 92   C. 118   D. 142

36.____

37. From the data given above, it can be seen that the overall height of a 2-ton truck is _____ inches.

    A. 47   B. 76   C. 79   D. 85

37.____

38.

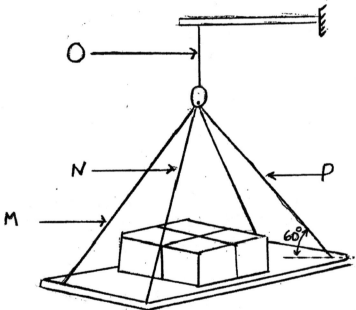

The above diagram shows a loaded sling suspended from a crane. The rope which carries the heaviest load is

    A. M   B. N   C. O   D. P

38.____

39. If the tray shown in the diagram at the right is being pushed in the direction shown by the arrows, it is MOST likely to move in the direction of the arrow shown in

39._____

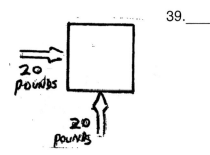

A.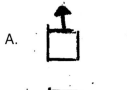

B.

C.

D.

40.

40._____

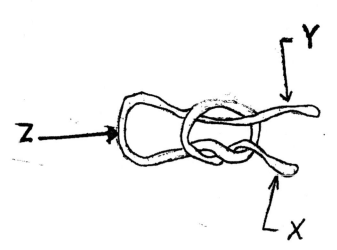

The above diagram shows a slip knot. The way this knot is nade, it would be CORRECT to say that the knot can be untied by pulling on line _____ while holding _____.

    A. X; line Z
    B. Y; line X
    C. X and line Y together; line Z
    D. Z; lines X and Y together

KEY (CORRECT ANSWERS)

1.	C	11.	A	21.	A	31.	C
2.	A	12.	B	22.	C	32.	B
3.	B	13.	C	23.	C	33.	D
4.	C	14.	A	24.	C	34.	A
5.	D	15.	D	25.	B	35.	D
6.	C	16.	A	26.	B	36.	C
7.	A	17.	C	27.	B	37.	D
8.	D	18.	C	28.	B	38.	C
9.	B	19.	C	29.	A	39.	B
10.	B	20.	D	30.	A	40.	B

EXAMINATION SECTION
TEST 1

DIRECTIONS: Each question or incomplete statement is followed by several suggested
answers or completions. Select the one that BEST answers the question or
completes the statement. *PRINT THE LETTER OF THE CORRECT ANSWER
IN THE SPACE AT THE RIGHT.*

Questions 1-8.

DIRECTIONS: Questions 1 through 8 involve tests on the fuse box arrangement shown
below. All tests are to be performed with a neon tester or a lamp test bank con-
sisting of two 6-watt, 120-volt lamps connected in series. Do not make any
assumptions about the conditions of the circuits. Draw your conclusions only
from the information obtained with the neon tester or the two-lamp test bank,
applied to the circuits as called for.

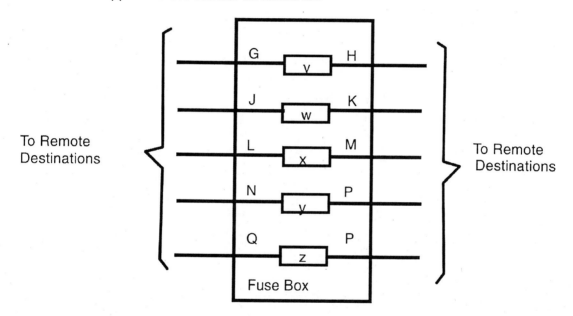

1.   The two lamp test bank is placed from point *G* to joint *J*, and both lamps light.   1._____
One of the lamps is momentarily removed from its socket; during that instant, the other
lamp in the series-connected test bank should

    A.   go dark   B.   get dimmer
    C.   remain at same brightness   D.   get brighter

2.   The test bank with two 60-watt, 120-volt lamps in series should be used on circuits with   2._____

    A.   wattages only from 60 to 120 watts
    B.   wattages only from 0 to 120 watts
    C.   voltages only from 120 to 240 volts
    D.   voltages only from 0 to 240 volts

3. The neon tester is placed from point *G* to point *J* and only one-half of the neon tester lights.
It should be concluded that

    A.   half of the tester has gone bad
    B.   a wire has become disconnected in the circuit
    C.   the voltage is AC
    D.   the voltage is DC

3.____

4. If both lamps in the test bank light when placed directly across one of the above fuses, it should be concluded that

    A.   the fuse is good
    B.   the fuse is blown
    C.   the fuse is overrated
    D.   further tests have to be made to determine the condition of the fuse

4.____

5. If the lamp test bank does not light when placed directly across one of the above fuses, it should be concluded that

    A.   the fuse is good
    B.   the fuse is blown
    C.   the fuse is overrated
    D.   further tests have to be made to determine the condition of the fuse

5.____

6. The lamp test bank lights when placed from point *G* to point *J* but does not light when placed from point *H* to point *J*.
It should be concluded that

    A.   the wire to point *H* has become disconnected
    B.   the wire to point *J* has become disconnected
    C.   fuse v is bad
    D.   fuse *w* is bad

6.____

7. The lamp test bank lights when placed from point *L* to point *N* but does not light when placed from point *M* to point *P*.
It should be concluded that

    A.   both fuses *x* and *y* are bad
    B.   either fuse *x* or fuse *y* is bad or both are bad
    C.   both fuses *x* and *y* are good
    D.   these tests do not indicate the condition of any fuse

7.____

8. The lamp test bank is placed from point *L* to point *N*, then from *N* to point *Q*, and finally from point *L* to point *Q*. In each case, both lamps light to full brightness.
It should be concluded that points *L*, *N*, and *Q* have

    A.   three-phase, 120 volts, AC, line-to-line
    B.   plus and minus 120 volts, DC
    C.   three-phase, 208 volts, AC
    D.   plus and minus 240 volts, DC

8.____

9. An automatic device used for regulating air temperature is a(n)   9.____

    A. rheostat   B. aquastat   C. thermostat   D. duostat

10. Assume that you have just completed a certain maintenance job which you feel is satis-   10.____
factory, but your foreman asks you to make certain changes.
The BEST procedure for you to follow is to

    A. request the foreman to assign this work to someone else
    B. have another maintainer verify that the job was done properly
    C. ask the foreman the reasons for the changes
    D. complain to the foreman's superior of this waste of time

11. The PROPER set of tools and equipment to be used to clean and adjust the ignition   11.____
points of an automobile consists of a

    A. screwdriver, feeler gauge, and point file
    B. wrench, micrometer, and sandpaper
    C. scraper, micrometer, and emery cloth
    D. V-block, pliers, and sandpaper

12. The voltage developed in each cell of an automobile battery is _____ volts.   12.____

    A. 2   B. 4   C. 6   D. 12

13. The one of the following tools that is NOT used to clear plumbing stoppages is a   13.____

    A. force-cup   B. drain auger
    C. snake   D. pick-out iron

14. Eyebolts are generally fastened to the shells of machinery in order to   14.____

    A. act as a leveling device
    B. facilitate lifting
    C. permit easy tagging of the equipment
    D. reinforce the machine shells

15. When grinding a weld smooth, it is MOST important to avoid   15.____

    A. grinding too slowly
    B. overheating the surrounding metal
    C. grinding away too much of the weld
    D. grinding after the weld has cooled off

16. A cold chisel whose head has become *mushroomed* should NOT be used because   16.____

    A. it is impossible to hit the head squarely
    B. the chisel will not cut accurately
    C. chips might fly from the head
    D. the chisel has lost its *temper*

17. The type of screwdriver specially made to be used in tight spots is the   17.____

    A. Phillips   B. offset
    C. square shank   D. truss

18. An indication that a fluorescent lamp in a fixture should be replaced is   18.____

    A. humming in the fixture
    B. the ends of the lamp remain black when the lamp is lit
    C. poor or slow starting
    D. the lamp does not shut off each time the OFF button is pressed

19. Asbestos is used as a covering on electrical wires to provide protection from   19.____

    A. high voltage   B. high temperatures
    C. water damage   D. electrolysis

20. Many electric power tools, such as drills, have a third conductor in the line cord which   20.____
should be connected to a grounded part of the power receptacle.
The reason for this is to

    A. have a spare wire in case one power wire should break
    B. strengthen the power lead so that it cannot be easily damaged
    C. protect the user of the tool from electrical shocks
    D. allow use of the tool for extended periods of time without overheating

21. Employees are responsible for the good care, proper maintenance, and serviceable con-   21.____
dition of the property issued or assigned for their use.
As used above, *serviceable condition* means the property is in a state where it is

    A. capable of being repaired   B. easily handled
    C. fit for use   D. least expensive

22. A brush that has been used in shellac should be cleaned by washing it in   22.____

    A. water   B. linseed oil
    C. lacquer thinner   D. alcohol

23. Excessive moisture on a surface being painted would MOST likely result in   23.____

    A. alligatoring   B. blistering
    C. cracking   D. sagging

24. In order to reverse the direction of rotation of a series motor, the   24.____

    A. connections to the armature should be reversed
    B. connections to both the armature and the series field should be reversed
    C. connections of the motor to the power lines should be reversed
    D. series field should be placed in shunt with the armature

25. A megger is an instrument used to measure   25.____

    A. capacitance   B. insulation resistance
    C. power   D. illumination levels

26. The first aid treatment for chemical burns on the skin is   26.____

    A. treatment with ointment and then bandaging
    B. washing with large quantities of water and then treating as heat burns
    C. treatment with a neutralizing agent and no bandaging
    D. application of sodium bicarbonate and then bandaging

27. The chemical MOST frequently used to clean drains clogged with grease is   27.____

    A. muriatic acid   B. soda ash
    C. ammonia   D. caustic soda

28. When tapping a blind hole in a steel plate, the FIRST type of tap to use is a _____ tap.   28.____

    A. plug   B. taper   C. lead   D. bottoming

29. A common handshaving tool used in woodwork is a(n)   29.____

    A. trammel   B. router   C. auger   D. plane

30. *Dressing* a grinding wheel refers to   30.____

    A. making the wheel thinner
    B. replacing with a new wheel
    C. repairing a crack in the wheel
    D. making the wheel round

31. The maintainer who is MOST valuable is the one who   31.____

    A. offers to do the heavy lifting
    B. asks many questions about the work
    C. listens to instructions and carries them out
    D. makes many suggestions on work procedures

32. Of the following, turpentine is used for thinning   32.____

    A. latex paint   B. red lead paint
    C. calcimine   D. shellac

33. Of the following, the hacksaw blade BEST suited for cutting thin-walled tubing is one which has _____ teeth/inch.   33.____

    A. 14   B. 18   C. 24   D. 32

34. Because of its weather-resistant properties, a varnish commonly used on exterior surfaces is _____ varnish.   34.____

    A. spar   B. flat   C. rubbing   D. hard oil

35. A trip spring or spring cylinder on a snow plow assembly is a device that   35.____

    A. absorbs the shock of impact when the plow strikes an obstacle in the road
    B. provides for snap-action in the lowering of the plow blade
    C. allows for quick removal or attachment of the snow plow supporting frame
    D. detaches the plow blade and lets it hang free when the plow blade is dragged backwards

36. The term *preventative maintenance* is used to identify a plan whereby   36.____

    A. equipment is serviced according to a regular schedule
    B. equipment is serviced as soon as it fails
    C. equipment is replaced as soon as it becomes obsolete
    D. all equipment is replaced periodically

37. The ratio of air to gasoline in an automobile engine is controlled by the   37._____

    A. gas filter   B. fuel pump
    C. carburetor   D. intake manifold

38. *Energizer* is another name given to the   38._____

    A. automobile battery   B. fluorescent fixture ballast
    C. battery charger   D. generator shunt field

39. Wearshoes may be found on   39._____

    A. circuit breakers   B. automobile brake systems
    C. snow plows   D. door sills

40. When moving heavy equipment by means of pipe rollers, it is MOST important to   40._____

    A. use solid steel rollers
    B. use rollers with different diameters
    C. see that the trailing roller does not slip out from under the equipment
    D. use more than three rollers at all times

41. The one of the following storage areas that is BEST for the storage of paint is one which is   41._____

    A. unheated and not ventilated
    B. cool and ventilated
    C. sunny and ventilated
    D. warm and not ventilated

42. The leverage that can be obtained with a wrench is determined mainly by the   42._____

    A. material of which the wrench is made
    B. gripping surface of the jaw
    C. length of the handle
    D. thickness of the wrench

43. A star drill is used to bore holes in   43._____

    A. steel   B. concrete   C. wood   D. sheet metal

44. The one of the following actions of a maintainer that is MOST likely to contribute to a good working relationship between him and his assistant is for him to   44._____

    A. observe the same rules of conduct that he expects his assistant to observe
    B. freely give advice on his assistant's personal problems
    C. always be frank and outspoken to his assistant in pointing out his faults
    D. expect his assistant to perform with equal efficiency on any job assigned

45. Three common types of windows are   45._____

    A. batten, casement, and awning
    B. batten, casement, and double-hung
    C. batten, double-hung, and awning
    D. casement, double-hung, and awning

46. A staircase has twelve risers, each 6 3/4" high. The TOTAL rise of the staircase is

    A. $6'2\frac{1}{4}"$　　　B. 6'9"　　　C. 7'0"　　　D. 7'3 3/4"

46.____

47. A twenty-foot straight ladder placed at an angle against a wall should be at a distance from the wall equal to _____ feet.

    A. 3　　　B. 5　　　C. 7　　　D. 9

47.____

48. Reflective sheeting traffic signs that have become dirty should be wiped with kerosene or gasoline FOLLOWED by a

    A. wiping with a soft cloth soaked in thin oil
    B. hand rub with very fine sandpaper
    C. wash with detergent and a rinse with water
    D. coating of shellac applied with a brush

48.____

49. A temporary wooden fence carrying red flags and built around an opening in a pavement to warn oncoming traffic is known as a

    A. batter board　　　　　　B. bulkhead
    C. bollard　　　　　　　　D. barricade

49.____

50. *Four-ply belted* is used to describe the construction of

    A. belt-drive pulleys
    B. auto tires
    C. electrical wiring insulation
    D. seat belts

50.____

―――――

KEY (CORRECT ANSWERS)

1.	A	11.	A	21.	C	31.	C	41.	B
2.	D	12.	A	22.	D	32.	B	42.	C
3.	D	13.	D	23.	B	33.	D	43.	B
4.	B	14.	B	24.	A	34.	A	44.	A
5.	D	15.	C	25.	B	35.	A	45.	D
6.	C	16.	C	26.	B	36.	A	46.	B
7.	B	17.	B	27.	D	37.	C	47.	B
8.	C	18.	B	28.	B	38.	A	48.	C
9.	C	19.	B	29.	D	39.	C	49.	D
10.	C	20.	C	30.	D	40.	C	50.	B

―――――

TEST 2

DIRECTIONS: Each question or incomplete statement is followed by several suggested answers or completions. Select the one that BEST answers the question or completes the statement. *PRINT THE LETTER OF THE CORRECT ANSWER IN THE SPACE AT THE RIGHT.*

1. An oil bath filter is MOST often used on a(n)

   A. air compressor   B. auto engine
   C. electric generator   D. steam boiler

1._____

2. A 3-ohm resistor placed across a 12-volt battery will dissipate _____ watts.

   A. 3   B. 4   C. 12   D. 48

2._____

3. Instead of using fuses, modern electric wiring uses

   A. quick switches   B. circuit breakers
   C. fusible links   D. lag blocks

3._____

4. The MOST common combination of gases used for welding is

   A. carbon dioxide and acetylene
   B. nitrogen and hydrogen
   C. oxygen and acetylene
   D. oxygen and hydrogen

4._____

5. If a wheel has turned through an angle of 180, then it has made _____ revolution(s).

   A. 1/4   B. 1/2   C. 1/8   D. 18

5._____

6. Sewer gas is prevented from backing up through a plumbing fixture by a

   A. water trap   B. return elbow
   C. check valve   D. float valve

6._____

7. Putty that is too stiff is made workable by adding

   A. gasoline   B. linseed oil
   C. water   D. lacquer thinner

7._____

8. A vertical wood member in the wall of a wood frame house is known as a

   A. A stringer   B. ridge member
   C. stud   D. header

8._____

9. A 10-to-1 step-down transformer has an input of 1 ampere at 120 volts AC. If the losses are negligible, the output of the transformer is _____ volts.

   A. 1 ampere at 12   B. .1 ampere at 1200
   C. 10 amperes at 12   D. 10 amperes at 120

9._____

10. An oscilloscope is an instrument used in

   A. measuring noise levels
   B. displaying waveforms of electrical signals
   C. indicating the concentrations of pollutants in air
   D. photographing high-speed events

10._____

11. Assume that a brake pedal of a truck goes to the floorboard when depressed. The one of the following that could cause this condition is

    A. a leak in the hydraulic lines
    B. a clogged hydraulic line
    C. scored drums
    D. glazed linings

11._____

12. The universal joints of an automobile are located on the

    A. suspension springs
    C. wheel cylinders
    B. steering linkages
    D. drive shaft

12._____

13. The MAIN purpose of a flexible coupling is to connect two shafts which are

    A. of different diameters
    C. not in exact alignment
    B. of different shapes
    D. of different material

13._____

14. When using a standard measuring micrometer, starting with a zero reading, one complete counterclockwise revolution of the sleeve will give a reading of _____ inch.

    A. .001   B. .010   C. .025   D. .250

14._____

15. If a nut is to be tightened to an exact specified value of inch-lbs., the wrench to use is a _____ wrench.

    A. spanner   B. box   C. lock-jaw   D. torque

15._____

16. Common permanent type anti-freezes for automobile cooling systems are MAINLY

    A. alcohol
    C. ethylene glycol
    B. methanol
    D. trychloroethylene

16._____

17. Plexiglas is also called

    A. mylar   B. lucite   C. isinglass   D. PVC

17._____

18. Long, curved lines are BEST cut in 1/4" plexiglas with a _____ saw.

    A. rip   B. jig   C. keyhole   D. coping

18._____

19. The specific gravity of storage battery cells can be measured with a(n)

    A. odometer   B. hydrometer   C. ammeter   D. dwell meter

19._____

20. A nail set is a tool used for

    A. straightening bent nails
    B. measuring nail sizes
    C. cutting nails to specified size
    D. driving a nail head into wood

20._____

21. To cut a number of 2" x 4" lengths of wood accurately at an angle of 45°, it is BEST to use a

    A. protractor   B. mitre-box   C. triangle   D. square

21._____

22. The type of fastener MOST commonly used when bolting to concrete uses a(n)   22.___

    A. expansion shield   B. U-bolt
    C. toggle bolt   D. turnbuckle

23. When an automobile engine does not start on a damp day, the trouble is MOST likely in   23.___
the _____ system.

    A. ignition   B. cooling   C. fuel   D. lubricating

24. The battery of an automobile is prevented from discharging back through the alternator   24.___
by the blocking action of the

    A. commutator   B. diodes   C. brushes   D. slip rings

25. The master cylinder in an automobile is actuated by the   25.___

    A. steering column   B. brake pedal
    C. clutch plate   D. cam shaft

26. The FINEST sandpaper from among the following is No.   26.___

    A. 3   B. 1   C. 2/0   D. 6/0

27. A screw whose head is buried below the surface of the wood that it is screwed into is said   27.___
to be

    A. countersunk   B. scalloped
    C. expanded   D. flushed

28. The one of the following devices which is used to measure angles is the   28.___

    A. caliper   B. protractor
    C. marking gauge   D. divider

29. Before a new oil stone is used, it should be   29.___

    A. heated   B. soaked in oil
    C. coated with shellac   D. washed with soapy water

30. Dies are used for   30.___

    A. threading the outside ends of metal pipes
    B. making sweated joints on lead pipes
    C. cutting nipples to exact lengths
    D. caulking cast-iron pipe joints

31. The energy stored by a storage battery is commonly given in   31.___

    A. volts   B. amperes
    C. ampere-hours   D. kilowatts

32. *Vapor lock* occurs in automobile   32.___

    A. gas tanks   B. crankcases
    C. transmissions   D. carburetors

33. A woodworking tool used to bore odd-size holes for which there is no standard auger bit is a(n)

    A. single twist auger   B. double twist auger
    C. expansive bit   D. straight fluted drill

33.____

34. Soap is sometimes applied to wood screws in order to

    A. prevent rust   B. make a tight fit
    C. make insertion easier   D. prevent wood splitting

34.____

35. On a long run of copper tubing, the tubing is often bent in the shape of a horseshoe rather than being run in a straight line.
The MAIN reason for this is to

    A. allow an excess that could be used in future repairs
    B. make it easier to install the tubing
    C. permit the tubing to expand and contract with changes in temperature
    D. eliminate the need for accurate measurements in cutting the tubing

35.____

36. Loss of seal water in a house water trap is prevented by the use of a

    A. drainage tee   B. faucet   C. hose bibb   D. vent

36.____

37. BX is a designation for a type of

    A. flexible armored electric cable
    B. flexible gas line
    C. rigid conduit
    D. electrical insulation

37.____

38. *WYE-WYE* and *DELTA-WYE* are two

    A. types of DC motor windings
    B. arrangements of 3-phase transformer connections
    C. types of electrical splices
    D. shapes of commutator bars

38.____

39. Green lumber should NOT be used in the building of scaffolding because it

    A. will not hold nails well
    B. easily splits when nailed
    C. may warp on drying
    D. is too expensive

39.____

40. *Scotchlite* ready-made traffic sign faces with heat-activated adhesive backings are applied to backing blanks by use of a

    A. temperature-controlled oven
    B. vacuum applicator
    C. hot water bath
    D. heated roller assembly

40.____

41. *Scotchcal* is a(n)

    A. reflective sheeting   B. epoxy protective paint
    C. fluorescent film   D. high temperature lubricant

41.____

42. Wooden ladders should NOT be painted because the paint   42.____

    A. is inflammable
    B. may cover defects in the wood
    C. makes the rungs slippery
    D. may deteriorate the wood

43. To prevent ladders from slipping, the bottoms of the ladder side rails are OFTEN fitted   43.____
with

    A. automatic locks   B. ladder shoes
    C. ladder hooks   D. stirrups

44. A bowline is   44.____

    A. the sag that a scaffold develops when men get on it
    B. a knot with a loop that does not run
    C. a temporary telephone wire strung during emergencies
    D. the reference line established in ditch excavations

45. A method sometimes used to prevent a pipe from buckling during a bending operation is   45.____
to

    A. bend the pipe very quickly
    B. keep the seam of the pipe on the outside of the bend
    C. nick the pipe at the center of the bend
    D. pack the inside of the pipe with sand

46. A rectifier changes   46.____

    A. DC to AC
    B. AC to DC
    C. single-phase power to three-phase power
    D. battery power to three-phase power

47. Continuity in a de-energized electrical circuit may be checked with a(n)   47.____

    A. voltmeter   B. ohmmeter   C. neon tester   D. rheostat

48. Of the following crankcase oils, the one that should be used in sub-zero weather is   48.____
SAE

    A. 10W   B. 20W   C. 20   D. 30

49. Caster in an automobile is an adjustment in the   49.____

    A. ignition system   B. drive-shaft
    C. rear differential   D. front suspension

50. If the spark plugs in an engine run too hot, the result is MOST likely that   50.____

    A. oil and carbon compounds will accumulate on the insulators
    B. the electrodes will wear rapidly
    C. the timing will be retarded
    D. the ignition coil may become damaged

KEY (CORRECT ANSWERS)

1. B	11. A	21. B	31. C	41. C
2. B	12. D	22. A	32. D	42. B
3. B	13. C	23. A	33. C	43. B
4. C	14. C	24. B	34. C	44. B
5. B	15. D	25. B	35. C	45. D
6. A	16. C	26. D	36. D	46. B
7. B	17. B	27. A	37. A	47. B
8. C	18. B	28. B	38. B	48. A
9. C	19. B	29. B	39. C	49. D
10. B	20. D	30. A	40. B	50. B

MECHANICAL APTITUDE
TOOLS AND THEIR USE

EXAMINATION SECTION
TEST 1

Questions 1-16.

DIRECTIONS: Questions 1 through 16 refer to the tools shown below. The numbers in the
answers refer to the numbers beneath the tools.
NOTE: These tools are NOT shown to scale

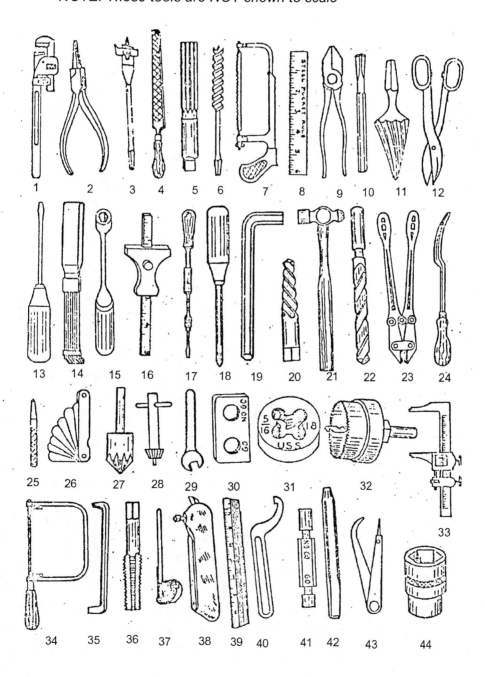

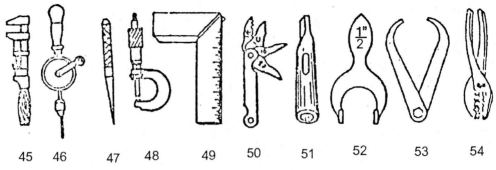

45   46   47   48   49   50   51   52   53   54

1. A 1" x 1" x 1/8" angle iron should be cut by using tool number   1._____

    A. 7   B. 12   C. 23   D. 42

2. To peen an iron rivet, you should use tool number   2._____

    A. 4   B. 7   C. 21   D. 43

3. The star "drill" is tool number   3._____

    A. 5   B. 10   C. 20   D. 22

4. To make holes in sheet metal for sheet metal screws, you should use tool number . 4._____

    A. 6   B. 10   C. 36   D. 46

5. To cut through a 3/8" diameter wire rope, you should use tool number   5._____

    A. 12   B. 23   C. 42   D. 54

6. To remove cutting burrs from the inside of a steel pipe, you should use tool number 6._____

    A. 5   B. 11   C. 14   D. 20

7. The depth of a bored hole may be measured MOST accurately with tool number   7._____

    A. 8   B. 16   C. 26   D. 41

8. If the marking on the blade of tool number 7 reads:12"-32", the 32 refers to the   8._____

    A. length   B. thickness   C. weight
    D. number of teeth per inch

9. If tool number 6 bears the mark "5", it should be used to drill holes having a diameter of 9._____

    A. 5/32"   B. 5/16"   C. 5/8"   D. 5"

10. To determine MOST quickly the number of threads per inch on a bolt, you should use tool 10._____
    number

    A. 8   B. 16   C. 26   D. 50

11. Wood screws, located in positions where the headroom does not permit the use of an 11._____
    ordinary screwdriver, may be removed by using tool number

    A. 17   B. 28   C. 35   D. 46

12. To remove a broken-off piece of 1/2" diameter pipe from a fitting, you should use tool number

    A. 5   B. 11   C. 20   D. 36

12.____

13. The outside diameter of a bushing may be measured MOST accurately with tool number

    A. 8   B. 26   C. 33   D. 43

13.____

14. To re-thread a stud hole in the casting of an elevator motor, you should use tool number

    A. 5   B. 20   C. 22   D. 36

14.____

15. To enlarge slightly a bored hole in a steel plate, you should use tool number

    A. 5   B. 11   C. 20   D. 36

15.____

16. The term "16 oz." should be applied to tool number

    A. 1   B. 12   C. 21   D. 42

16.____

KEYS (CORRECT ANSWERS)

1.	A	9.	B
2.	C	10.	D
3.	B	11.	C
4.	D	12.	C
5.	B	13.	C
6.	B	14.	D
7.	B	15.	A
8.	D	16.	C

TEST 2

Questions 1-11.

DIRECTIONS: Questions 1 through 11 refer to the instruments listed below. Each instrument is listed with an identifying number in front of it.

1 - Hygrometer	6 - Oscilloscope	11 - 6-foot folding rule
2 - Ammeter	7 - Frequency meter	12 - Architect's scale
3 - Voltmeter	8 - Micrometer	13 - Planimeter
4 - Wattmeter	9 - Vernier calliper	14 - Engineer's scale
5 - Megger	10 - Wire gage	15 - Ohmmeter

1. The instrument that should be used to *accurately* measure the resistance of a 4,700-ohm resistor is number   1.____

   A. 3   B. 4   C. 7   D. 15

2. To measure the current in an electrical circuit, the instrument that should be used is number   2.____

   A. 2   B. 7   C. 8   D. 15

3. To measure the insulation resistance of a rubber-covered electrical cable, the instrument that should be used is number   3.____

   A. 4   B. 5   C. 8   D. 15

4. An AC motor is hooked up to a power distribution box. In order to check the voltage at the motor terminals, the instrument that should be used is number   4.____

   A. 2   B. 3   C. 4   D. 7

5. To measure the shaft diameter of a motor *accurately* to one-thousandth of an inch, the instrument that should be used is number   5.____

   A. 8   B. 10   C. 11   D. 14

6. The instrument that should be used to determine whether 25 Hz. or 60 Hz. is present in an electrical circuit is number   6.____

   A. 4   B. 5   C. 7   D. 8

7. Of the following, the *proper* instrument to use to determine the diameter of the conductor of a piece of electrical hookup wire is number   7.____

   A. 10   B. 11   C. 12   D. 14

8. The amount of electrical power being used in a balanced three-phase circuit should be measured with number   8.____

   A. 2   B. 3   C. 4   D. 5

9. The electrical wave form at a given point in an electronic circuit can be observed with number   9.____

   A. 2   B. 3   C. 6   D. 7

10. The *proper* instrument to use for measuring the width of a door is number   10.____

    A. 11   B. 12   C. 13   D. 14

11. A one-inch hole with a tolerance of plus or minus three-thousandths is reamed in a steel   11.____
block. The *proper* instrument to accurately check the diameter of the hole is number

    A. 8   B. 9   C. 11   D. 14

12. An oilstone is LEAST likely to be used correctly to sharpen a   12.____

    A. scraper   B. chisel   C. knife   D. saw

13. To cut the ends of a number of lengths of wood at an angle of 45 degrees, it would be   13.____
BEST to use a

    A. mitre-box   B. protractor   C. triangle   D. wooden rule

14. A gouge is a tool used for   14.____

    A. planing wood smooth   B. grinding metal
    C. drilling steel   D. chiseling wood

15. Holes are usually countersunk when installing   15.____

    A. carriage bolts   B. lag screws
    C. flat-head screws   D. square nuts

16. A tool that is *generally* used to slightly elongate a round hole in scrap-iron is a   16.____

    A. rat-tail file   B. reamer   C. drill   D. rasp

17. When the term "10-24" is used to specify a machine screw, the number 24 refers to the   17.____

    A. number of screws per pound   B. diameter of the screw
    C. length of the screw   D. number of threads per inch

18. If you were unable to tighten a nut by means of a ratchet wrench because, although the   18.____
nut turned on with the forward movement of the wrench, it turned off with the backward
movement, you should

    A. make the nut hand-tight before using the wrench
    B. reverse the ratchet action
    C. put a few drops of oil on the wrench
    D. use a different socket in the handle

19. If you were installing a long wood screw and found you were unable to drive this screw   19.____
more than three-quarters of its length by the use of a properly-fitting straight-handled
screwdriver, the *proper* SUBSEQUENT action would be for you to

    A. take out the screw and put soap on it
    B. change to the use of a screwdriver-bit and brace
    C. take out the screw and drill a shorter hole before redriving
    D. use a pair of pliers on the blade of the screwdriver

20. Good practice requres that the end of a pipe to be installed in a plumbing system be reamed to remove the inside burr after it has been cut to length. The *purpose* of this reaming is to

    A.   restore the original inside diameter of the pipe at the end
    B.   remove loose rust
    C.   make the threading of the pipe easier
    D.   finish the pipe accurately to length

20.____

KEYS (CORRECT ANSWERS)

1.	D	11.	B
2.	A	12.	D
3.	B	13.	A
4.	B	14.	D
5.	A	15.	C
6.	C	16.	A
7.	A	17.	D
8.	C	18.	A
9.	C	19.	A
10.	A	20.	A

SAFETY
EXAMINATION SECTION
TEST 1

DIRECTIONS: Each question or incomplete statement is followed by several suggested answers or completions. Select the one that BEST answers the question or completes the statement. *PRINT THE LETTER OF THE COREECT ANSWER IN THE SPACE AT THE RIGHT.*

1. When carrying pipe, employees are cautioned against lifting with the fingers inserted in the ends.
    The PROBABLE reason for this caution is to avoid the possibility of

    A. dropping and damaging pipe
    B. getting dirt and perspiration on the inside of the pipe
    C. cutting the fingers on the edge of the pipe
    D. straining finger muscles

1.____

2. The MOST common cause for a workman to lose his balance and fall when working from an extension ladder is

    A. too much spring in the ladder
    B. sideways sliding of the top
    C. exerting a heavy pull on an object which gives suddenly
    D. working on something directly behind the ladder

2.____

3. It is NOT necessary to wear protective goggles when

    A. drilling rivet holes in a steel beam
    B. sharpening tools on a power grinder
    C. welding a steel plate to a pipe column
    D. laying up a cinder block partition

3.____

4. On your first day on the job as a helper, you are assigned to work with a maintainer. During the course of the work, you realize that the maintainer is about to violate a basic safety rule.
    In this case, the BEST thing for you to do is to

    A. immediately call it to his attention
    B. say nothing until he actually violates the rule and then call it to his attention
    C. say nothing, but later report this action to the foreman
    D. walk away from him so that you will not become involved

4.____

5. Telephones are located alongside of the tracks for emergency use. The locations of these telephones are indicated by blue lights.
    The reason for selecting this color rather than green is that

    A. a blue light can be seen for greater distances
    B. blue lights are easier to buy
    C. green cannot be seen by a person who is color-blind
    D. green lights are used for train signals

5.____

6. If it is necessary to lift up and hold one heavy part of a piece of equipment with a pinch   6.____
bar so that there is enough clearance to work with the hands under the part, one IMPOR-
TANT precaution is to

    A. wear gloves
    B. watch the bar to be ready if it slips
    C. work as fast as possible
    D. insert a temporary block to hold the part

7. The MOST important reason for insisting on neatness in maintenance quarters is that it   7.____

    A. increases the available storage space
    B. makes for good employee morale
    C. prevents tools from becoming rusty
    D. decreases the chances of accidents to employees

8. There are many steel ladders and stairways for the use of maintenance workers.   8.____
Their GREATEST danger is that they

    A. have sharp edges causing cuts
    B. are slippery when greasy and wet
    C. cause colds
    D. have no *give* and thus cause fatigue

9. When using a brace and bit to bore a hole completely through a partition, it is MOST   9.____
important to

    A. lean heavily on the brace and bit
    B. maintain a steady turning speed all through the job
    C. have the body in a position that will not be easily thrown off balance
    D. reverse the direction of the bit at frequent intervals

10. Flux is used when soldering two pieces of sheet metal together in order to   10.____

    A. conduct the heat of the soldering iron to the sheets
    B. lower the melting point of the solder
    C. glue the solder to the sheets
    D. protect the sheet metal from oxidizing when heated by the soldering iron

11. A rule of the transit system states that in walking on the track, walk opposite the direction   11.____
of traffic on that track if possible.
By logical reasoning, the PRINCIPAL safety idea behind this rule is that the man on
the track

    A. is more likely to see an approaching train
    B. will be seen more readily by the motorman
    C. need not be as careful
    D. is better able to judge the speed of the train

12. An outstanding cause of accidents is the improper use of tools.   12.____
The MOST helpful conclusion you can draw from this statement is that

    A. most tools are defective
    B. many accidents involving the use of tools occur because of poor working habits

C. most workers are poorly trained
D. many accidents involving the use of tools are unavoidable

13. An employee is required to make a written report of any unusual occurrence promptly. The BEST reason for requiring promptness is that 13.____

A. it helps prevent similar occurrences
B. the employee is less likely to forget details
C. there is always a tendency to do a better job under pressure
D. the report may be too long if made at an employee"s convenience

14. There are a few workers who are seemingly prone to accidents and who, regardless of their assigned job, have a higher accident rate than the average worker. If your co-worker is known to be such an individual, the BEST course for you to pursue would be to 14.____

A. do most of the assigned work yourself
B. refuse to work with this individual
C. provide him with a copy of all rules and regulations
D. personally check all safety precautions on each job

15. When summoning an ambulance for an injured person, it is MOST important to give the 15.____

A. name of the injured person
B. nature of the injuries
C. cause of the accident
D. location of the injured person

16. The MOST likely cause of accidents involving minor injuries is 16.____

A. careless work practices
B. lack of safety devices
C. inferior equipment and materials
D. insufficient safety posters

17. In an accident report, the information which may be MOST useful in decreasing the recurrence of similar-type accidents is the 17.____

A. extent of injuries sustained
B. time the accident happened
C. number of people involved
D. cause of the accident

18. Before a newly-riveted connection can be approved, the rivets should be struck with a light hammer in order to 18.____

A. improve the shape of the rivet heads
B. knock off any rust or burnt metal
C. detect any loose rivets
D. give the rivets a tighter fit

19. If the feet of a ladder are found to be resting on a slightly uneven surface, it would be 19.____
BEST to

   A. move the ladder to an entirely different location
   B. even up the feet of the ladder with a small wedge
   C. get two men to bolster the ladder while it is being climbed
   D. get another ladder that is more suitable to the conditions

20. It would be POOR practice to hold a piece of wood in your hands or lap while you are 20.____
tightening a screw in the wood because

   A. the wood would probably split
   B. sufficient leverage cannot be obtained
   C. the screwdriver may bend
   D. you might injure yourself

21. If a man on a job has to report an accident to the office by telephone, he should request 21.____
the name of the person taking the call and also note the time.
The reason for this precaution is to fix responsibility for the

   A. entire handling of the accident thereafter
   B. accuracy of the report
   C. recording of the report
   D. preparation of the final written report

22. Employees of the transit system whose work requires them to enter upon the tracks are 22.____
warned not to wear loose-fitting clothes.
The MOST important reason for this warning is that loose-fitting clothes may

   A. tear more easily than snug-fitting clothes
   B. give insufficient protection against dust
   C. catch on some projection of a passing train
   D. interfere when the men are using heavy tools

23. In case of accident, employees who witnessed the accident are required to make INDI- 23.____
VIDUAL written reports on prescribed forms as soon as possible.
The MOST logical reason for requiring such individual reports rather than a single,
joint report signed by all witnesses is that the individual reports are

   A. *less* likely to be lost at the same time
   B. *more* likely to result in reducing the number of accidents
   C. *less* likely to contain unnecessary information
   D. *more* likely to give the complete picture

24. The logical reason that certain employees who work on the tracks carry small parts in 24.____
fiber pails rather than in steel pails is that fiber pails

   A. can't be dented by rough usage
   B. do not conduct electricity
   C. are stronger
   D. can't rust

25. Maintenance workers whose duties require them to work on the tracks generally work in   25.____
   pairs.
   The LEAST likely of the following possible reasons for this practice is that

   A. the men can help each other in case of accident
   B. it protects against vandalism
   C. some of the work requires two men
   D. there is usually too much equipment for one man to carry

———

KEY (CORRECT ANSWERS)

1.	C	11.	A
2.	C	12.	B
3.	D	13.	B
4.	A	14.	D
5.	D	15.	D
6.	D	16.	A
7.	D	17.	D
8.	B	18.	C
9.	C	19.	B
10.	D	20.	D

21.	C
22.	C
23.	D
24.	B
25.	B

———

TEST 2

DIRECTIONS: Each question or incomplete statement is followed by several suggested answers or completions. Select the one that BEST answers the question or completes the statement. *PRINT THE LETTER OF THE CORRECT ANSWER IN THE SPACE AT THE RIGHT.*

1. Safety-mindedness cannot be achieved by command; it must be developed. Assume that you will be responsible for informing and training your subordinates in proper safety procedures.
   Which of the following methods is the MOST effective means of developing proper concern for safety among your subordinates?

   A.   Award prizes for the best safety slogans
   B.   Issue monthly safety bulletins
   C.   Establish a safety suggestion program
   D.   Hold periodic, informal group meetings on safety

1.____

2. Of the following, the MAIN purpose of a safety training program for employees is to

   A.   fix the blame for accidents
   B.   describe accidents which have occurred
   C.   hold the employees responsible for unsafe working conditions
   D.   make the employees aware of the basic causes of accidents

2.____

3. When administering first aid to a person suffering from shock as a result of an accident, of the following, it is MOST important to

   A.   cover the person and keep him warm
   B.   apply artificial respiration
   C.   prop him up in a sitting position
   D.   massage the person in order to aid blood circulation

3.____

4. Assume you have just been appointed. You notice that certain equipment which is assigned to you is defective and that use of this equipment may eventually result in unnecessary costs and perhaps injury to you.
   The BEST thing for you to do is to

   A.   speak to the maintenance men in the project about repairing the equipment
   B.   discuss the matter with your foreman
   C.   mind your own business since you have just been appointed
   D.   speak to other workers and find out if they had any experience with defective equipment

4.____

5. Assume you are working in a project building and one of the housing caretakers has just been seriously injured in an accident in the slop sink room.
   Your FIRST concern should be to

   A.   help the injured man
   B.   find the cause of the accident
   C.   report the accident to your foreman
   D.   report the accident to the caretaker's boss

5.____

6. Assume a mass of extension cords plugged into one outlet in a shop results in overload-   6._____
   ing the electrical circuit and causes a fire.
   Which of the following types of extinguisher should be used to put out the fire?

   A. Carbon dioxide (CO_2)   B. Water
   C. Soda acid   D. Carbon tetrachloride

7. Manufacturers of chemicals usually recommend that special precautions be taken when   7._____
   the chemicals are used.
   Of the following, which one would a manufacturer be LEAST likely to recommend?

   A. Wear leather gloves
   B. Wear a respirator
   C. Wear safety goggles
   D. Have a first aid kit available

Questions 8-10.

DIRECTIONS: Questions 8 through 10 consist of groups of statements that have to do with
               safety precautions and procedures. Choose the statement in each group that
               is NOT correct.

8. A. The label on the original container of the pesticide should be read before each use.   8._____
    B. Pest control equipment should be cleaned regularly.
    C. Whenever there is a choice of chemicals, the chemical which is less hazardous
        to humans should be used at all times.
    D. For the transfer of concentrates from drums, either threaded taps or drum pumps
        should be used.

9. A. Do not use a petroleum base on an asphalt tile floor.   9._____
    B. Do not spray oil base sprays on material colored with oil soluble dyes.
    C. Do not use respirators.
    D. Do not use pesticides which are highly poisonous to mammals.

10. (The following statements deal with disposal of empty containers which hold highly toxic   10._____
    organic phosphate insecticides.)

    A. Do not reuse these containers.
    B. Pour one pint of water into the empty container, add bicarbonate of soda, and bury
        the container of rinse solution at least 18 inches below ground.
    C. Wet all inner surfaces with the proper rinse solution.
    D. Punch holes in the top and bottom of the can, crush the can, and bury deeply in an
        isolated location.

11. A good first-aid treatment to administer to a man who has apparently been rendered   11._____
    unconscious by a high voltage shock would be to

    A. give him a stimulant by mouth
    B. apply artificial respiration if he is not breathing
    C. apply artificial respiration as a precautionary measure even if he is breathing
    D. keep him warm and comfortable

12. A contributing cause present in practically all accidents is 12.____

    A. failure to give close attention to the job at hand
    B. lack of cooperation among the men in a gang
    C. failure to place the right man in the right job
    D. use of improper tools

13. Safety requires that wood ladders be unpainted. 13.____
The PROBABLE reason for this is that paint

    A. is inflammable
    B. may deteriorate wood
    C. makes ladder rungs slippery
    D. may cover cracks or defects

14. If you notice one of your helpers doing a job in an unsafe manner and he tells you that 14.____
this is the way the maintainer told him to do it, you should FIRST

    A. speak to this maintainer and find out if the helper was telling you the truth
    B. reprimand the helper for violating safety rules
    C. question this maintainer to see if he knows the safe way to do the job
    D. show the helper the correct method and see that he does the job properly

15. If a person has a deep puncture in his finger caused by a sharp nail, the BEST immedi- 15.____
ate first-aid procedure would be to

    A. encourage bleeding by exerting pressure around the injured area
    B. stop all bleeding
    C. prevent air from reaching the wound
    D. probe the wound for steel particles

16. It is MOST important to give complete details of an accident on the accident report 16.____
because this will

    A. cause the injured employee to be more careful in the future
    B. keep supervision informed of the working conditions
    C. help in the defense against spurious compensation claims
    D. provide information to help avoid future accidents

17. A transit employee equipped with only a white flashlight, who wishes to stop a train 17.____
because of an emergency, should face the train and wave the light in a

    A. vertical line
    B. vertical circle
    C. horizontal line
    D. forward and backward direction

18. The employee who opens a first-aid kit must make an immediate report on a prescribed 18.____
form.
Such report would NOT show the

    A. name of the employee opening the kit
    B. last previous date on which the kit was used

C. purpose for which the materials therein were used
D. amount of first aid material used

19. Carbon tetrachloride fire extinguishers have been replaced by dry chemical fire extin-   19.____
guishers MAINLY because the carbon tetrachloride is

A. toxic
B. not as effective
C. frequently pilfered for cleaning purposes
D. not readily available

20. The BEST first-aid for a man who has no external injury but is apparently suffering from   20.____
internal injury due to an accident is to

A. take him immediately to a doctor's office
B. administer a stimulant
C. cover him with a blanket and immediately summon a doctor or ambulance
D. administer artificial respiration

21. While your men were working on the plumbing of a station toilet, a passenger tripped   21.____
over some of your material on the platform.
In making a report of the accident, the LEAST necessary item to include is the

A. time of day
B. distance from the entrance turnstile to the toilet
C. date of occurrence
D. condition of the platform when the accident occurred

22. All employees witnessing an accident are required to make a written report as soon as   22.____
possible describing what they witnessed.
The MOST likely reason for requiring these reports in writing and as soon as possible
is to

A. make sure no witnesses are overlooked
B. be able to correct the reports without delay
C. get as many facts as possible on record before they are forgotten
D. relieve supervision of the time consuming job of verbally questioning all witnesses

23. Of the following, the type of fire extinguisher which should be used on electrical fires is   23.____
the _____ type.

A. foam   B. soda-acid
C. pumped-water   D. dry chemical

24. The PRIMARY purpose of an emergency alarm is to   24.____

A. test circuits to see if they are alive
B. provide a means of removing power from the third rail
C. inform the trainmaster that trains cannot run in his zone
D. inform maintenance crews working on the tracks that an emergency exists

25. In regard to flagging signals, which of the following statements is TRUE?   25.____

    A. A red flag must never be used to give a proceed signal to a motorman.

    B. Under all conditions, only a red flag or lamp can be used as a signal to the motorman to stop the train.

    C. After stopping a train, if a flagman wishes to signal the motorman to resume his normal speed, he should wave a yellow flag.

    D. Under normal flagging conditions, moving a white light up and down slowly is a signal to the motorman to resume normal speed and that the motorman should be prepared to stop within his range of vision.

———

KEY (CORRECT ANSWERS)

1.	D		11.	B
2.	D		12.	A
3.	A		13.	D
4.	B		14.	D
5.	A		15.	A
6.	A		16.	D
7.	A		17.	C
8.	C		18.	B
9.	C		19.	A
10.	B		20.	C

21.	B
22.	C
23.	D
24.	B
25.	A

———

READING COMPREHENSION
UNDERSTANDING AND INTERPRETING WRITTEN MATERIAL
EXAMINATION SECTION
TEST 1

DIRECTIONS: Each question or Incomplete statement is followed by several suggested answers or completions. Select the one that BEST answers the question or completes the statement. *PRINT THE LETTER OF THE CORRECT ANSWER IN THE SPACE AT THE RIGHT.*

Questions 1-10.

DIRECTIONS: Questions 1 through 10 are to be answered on the basis of the description of an incident given below. Read the description carefully before answering these questions.

DESCRIPTION OF INCIDENT

On Tuesday, October 8, at about 4:00 P.M., bus operator Sam Bell, Badge No. 3871, whose accident record was perfect, was operating his half-filled bus, No. 4392Y, northbound and on schedule along Dean Street. At this time, a male passenger who was apparently intoxicated started to yell and to use loud and profane language. The bus driver told this passenger to be quiet or to get off the bus. The passenger said that he would not be quiet but indicated that he wanted to get off the bus by moving toward the front door exit. When he reached the front of the bus, which at the time was in motion, the intoxicated passenger slapped the bus operator on the back and pulled the steering wheel sharply. This action caused the bus to sideswipe a passenger automobile coming from the opposite direction before the operator could stop the bus. The sideswiped car was a red 2007 Pontiac 2-door convertible, License 6416-KN, driven by Albert Holt. The bus driver kept the doors of his bus closed and blew the horn vigorously. The horn blowing was quickly answered as Sergeant Henry Burns, Badge No. 1208, and Patrolman Joe Cross, Badge No. 24643, happened to be following a few cars behind the bus in police car No. 736. The intoxicated passenger, who gave his name as John Doe, was placed under arrest, and Patrolman Cross took the names of witnesses while Sergeant Burns recorded the necessary vehicular information. Investigation showed that no one was injured in the accident and that the entire damage to the automobile was having its side slightly pushed in.

1.   From the information given, it can be reasoned that   1.____

    A.   it was just beginning to rain
    B.   Dean Street is a two-way street
    C.   there were mostly women shoppers on the bus
    D.   most seats in the bus were filled

2.   The name of the policeman who was riding in the police car with the sergeant was   2.____

    A. Cross   B. Bell   C. Holt   D. Burns

3. From the description, it is evident that the passenger automobile was traveling   3.____

    A. north   B. south   C. east   D. west

4. It is logical to conclude that the passenger automobile was damaged on its   4.____

    A. front end   B. rear end
    C. right side   D. left side

5. A fact concerning the intoxicated passenger that is clearly stated in the above description is that he   5.____

    A. was intoxicated when he got on the bus
    B. hit a fellow passenger
    C. pulled the steering wheel sharply
    D. was not arrested

6. The bus operator called the attention of the police by   6.____

    A. sideswiping an oncoming car
    B. yelling and using profane language
    C. blowing his horn vigorously
    D. stopping a police car coming from the opposite direction

7. A reasonable conclusion that can be drawn from the above description is that   7.____

    A. the name John Doe was fictitious
    B. the sideswiped automobile was from out of town
    C. some of the passengers on the bus were injured
    D. the bus operator tried to put the intoxicated passenger off the bus

8. The number of the police car involved in the incident was   8.____

    A. 4392Y   B. 6416-KN   C. 1208   D. 736

9. From the facts stated, it is obvious that the bus operator was   9.____

    A. behind schedule
    B. driving too close to the center of the street
    C. discourteous to the intoxicated passenger
    D. a good driver

10. It is clearly stated that the   10.____

    A. sideswiped automobile was a blue sedan
    B. bus driver kept the bus doors closed until the police came
    C. incident happened on a Thursday
    D. police sergeant took down the names of witnesses

Questions 11-20.

DIRECTIONS: Questions 11 through 20 are to be answered on the basis of the paragraph below covering cleaning supplies. Refer to this paragraph when answering these questions.

CLEANING SUPPLIES

Certain amounts of cleaning supplies are used each week at each station of the Transit Authority. The following information applies to a station of average size. For cleaning floors, tiles, and toilets, approximately 14 pounds of soap powder is used each week. A scouring powder is used to clean unusually difficult stains, and approximately 1 1/2 pounds is used in a week. A disinfectant solution is used for cleaning telephone alcoves, toilets, and booth floors, and approximately 1 quart of undiluted disinfectant is used each week. To make a regular strength disinfectant solution, 1/4 ounce of undiluted disinfectant is added to 14 gallons of water. One pint of lemon oil is used each week to polish metal surfaces in booths and in other station areas.

11. In a period of 4 weeks, the amount of soap powder that is used at the average station is MOST NEARLY _____ pounds.　　11._____

　　A. 48　　　　　B. 52　　　　　C. 56　　　　　D. 60

12. In a period of 1 year, the amount of scouring powder that is used at the average station is MOST NEARLY _____ pounds.　　12._____

　　A. 26　　　　　B. 52　　　　　C. 64　　　　　D. 78

13. If a certain large station uses 1 1/2 times the soap powder that an average station uses, then the larger station uses MOST NEARLY _____ pounds a week.　　13._____

　　A. 14　　　　　B. 21　　　　　C. 24　　　　　D. 28

14. To make a regular strength disinfectant solution, the number of ounces of undiluted disinfectant that should be added to 3 gallons of water is　　14._____

　　A. 4　　　　　B. 3/4　　　　　C. 1　　　　　D. 1 1/4

15. To make a double strength disinfectant solution, the number of ounces of undiluted disinfectant that should be added to 3 gallons of water is　　15._____

　　A. 4　　　　　B. 3/4　　　　　C. 1　　　　　D. 1 1/2

16. In a period of 4 weeks, the amount of lemon oil that is used at the average station is _____ gallon(s).　　16._____

　　A. 1/4　　　　　B. 4　　　　　C. 1　　　　　D. 1 1/2

17. In a period of one year, the amount of soap powder that is used at 5 average stations is MOST NEARLY _____ pounds.　　17._____

　　A. 260　　　　　B. 728　　　　　C. 3,640　　　　　D. 5,260

18. To clean a station that is difficult to remove, it would be BEST for a porter to use　　18._____

　　A. soap powder　　　　　　　　　　B. scouring powder
　　C. disinfectant solution　　　　　　D. lemon oil

19. Lemon oil should be used for

    A. scouring
    B. regular cleaning
    C. polishing metal surfaces
    D. disinfecting

19._____

20. If a smaller than average station uses 3/4 of the amount of scouring powder than an average station uses, then in one week the amount of scouring powder used at the smaller station is MOST NEARLY _____ pound(s).

    A. 7/8   B. 1   C. 1 1/8   D. I 1/4

20._____

Questions 21-25.

DIRECTIONS: Questions 21 through 25, inclusive, are to be answered on the basis of the bus cleaning instructions below, which should be performed in the order given. Read the instructions carefully before answering these questions.

    1.   SPRAY wheels and mud guards with hand water hose to remove loose dirt.
    2.   SCRUB mud guards with brush and cleaner.
    3.   SCRUB wheels with brush and cleaner.
    4.   SCRAPE grease from wheels with hand scraper.
    5.   RINSE wheels and mud guards with hand water hose.

21. The cleaning instructions which involve the same parts of the bus are

    A. 1 and 2   B. 1 and 3   C. 2 and 4   D. 1 and 5

21._____

22. The scraping takes place

    A. *after* both the spraying and rinsing
    B. *after* the rinsing but before the scrubbing
    C. *before* both the scrubbing and rinsing
    D. *before* the rinsing but after the spraying

22._____

23. The hand water hose is NOT used to remove the grease because water

    A. cannot remove the grease properly
    B. would injure the motor
    C. has to be used as cleaner solution
    D. is used only for spraying

23._____

24. The brush is used in connection with operations

    A. 1 and 2   B. 2 and 3   C. 3 and 4   D. 4 and 5

24._____

25. Loose dirt is removed by

    A. scraping   B. scrubbing   C. spraying   D. rinsing

25._____

KEY (CORRECT ANSWERS)

1. B	11. C
2. A	12. D
3. B	13. B
4. D	14. A
5. C	15. C
6. C	16. B
7. A	17. C
8. D	18. B
9. D	19. C
10. B	20. C

21. D
22. D
23. A
24. B
25. C

———

TEST 2

DIRECTIONS: Each question or incomplete statement is followed by several suggested answers or completions. Select the one that BEST answers the question or completes the statement. *PRINT THE LETTER OF THE CORRECT ANSWER IN THE SPACE AT THE RIGHT.*

Questions 1-8.

DIRECTIONS: Questions 1 through 8 are to be answered on the basis of the information contained in the safety rules given. Read these rules carefully before answering these questions.

SAFETY RULES FOR EMPLOYEES WORKING ON TRACKS

Always carry a hand lantern whenever walking a track and walk opposite to the direction of the traffic on that particular track, if possible.

At all times when walking track, take note of and be prepared to use the spaces available for safety, clear of passing trains. Be careful to avoid those positions where clearance is insufficient.

Employees are particularly cautioned with respect to sections of track on which regular operation of passenger trains may at times be abandoned and which are used as lay-up tracks. Such tracks are likely to be used at any and irregular times by special trains such as work trains, lay-up trains, etc. At no time can any section of track be assumed to be definitely out of service, and employees must observe, when on or near tracks, the usual precautions regardless of any assumption as to operating schedules.

1. Safety rules are MOST useful because they

    A. make it unnecessary to think
    B. prevent carelessness
    C. are a guide to avoid common dangers
    D. make the workman responsible for any accident

1.____

2. A trackman walking a section of track should walk

    A. to the left of the tracks
    B. to the right of the tracks
    C. in the direction of traffic
    D. opposite to the direction of traffic

2.____

3. One precaution a trackman should ALWAYS take is to

    A. have power turned off on those tracks where he is walking
    B. place a red lantern behind him when walking back
    C. wave his lantern constantly when walking track
    D. note nearby safety spaces

3.____

4. Special trains are GENERALLY   4._____

    A. passenger trains on regular schedule
    B. express trains on local tracks
    C. work trains or lay-up trains
    D. trains going opposite to traffic

5. A trackman walking track should   5._____

    A. stay clear of all safety spaces
    B. expect all trains to be on schedule
    C. avoid tracks used by passenger trains
    D. carry a hand lantern

6. On sections of track not used for regular passenger trains, a trackman should   6._____

    A. follow the rules governing tracks in passenger train operation
    B. assume that no trains will be operating
    C. walk in the direction of traffic
    D. disregard the usual precautions

7. Safety spaces are provided in the subway for   7._____

    A. lay-up trains   B. passing trains
    C. employee's use   D. easier walking

8. A trackman would NOT expect lay-up tracks to be used by   8._____

    A. special trains
    B. trains carrying passengers
    C. work trains
    D. lay-up trains

Questions 9-17.

DIRECTIONS: Questions 9 through 17 are to be answered on the basis of the porters' instructions given below. Read these instructions carefully before answering these questions

PORTERS' INSTRUCTIONS

Railroad porters are prohibited from entering the token booths except for cleaning or relieving the railroad clerk. When the cleaning or relief has been completed, porters must leave booths immediately and must not loiter in or around the booths. Porters must not leave their equipment or supplies, such as dust pans, brooms, soap, etc., on any stairway, passageway, walkway, or in any place which may result in a hazard to passengers or others. Whenever an accident occurs on the station where the porter is assigned, he must submit a report on the prescribed form, always giving the condition of the place where the accident occurred. Porters must be in prescribed uniforms ready for work when reporting *on* and *off* duty.

9. The instructions would indicate that the porters' PRINCIPAL duty is to 9._____

   A. make out accident reports
   B. wear a uniform
   C. relieve the railroad clerk
   D. keep the station clean

10. Porters are permitted to enter token booths 10._____

   A. any time they wish
   B. after finishing cleaning
   C. to relieve the railroad clerk
   D. to avoid loitering elsewhere

11. The PROBABLE reason why porters cannot stay in the token booth even if their regular 11._____
    work is done is because

   A. they have a regular porters' room
   B. they are not trusted
   C. there is no room
   D. passengers may complain

12. Porters are used to relieve railroad clerks MAINLY because 12._____

   A. they need the training
   B. they are conveniently available
   C. their regular work is hard
   D. their work is similar

13. In submitting a report on an accident, the porter is instructed to 13._____

   A. explain the cause
   B. use any convenient paper
   C. give the condition of the place
   D. telephone it to his superior

14. The MOST likely reason for having special uniforms for porters is to 14._____

   A. give them authority
   B. avoid a variety of unpresentable clothes
   C. save them money
   D. permit them to enter without paying fare

15. Evidently, porters must be careful where they leave their equipment or supplies to avoid 15._____

   A. spoilage   B. theft
   C. loss of time   D. injury to passengers

16. Such instructions to porters are NECESSARY because 16._____

   A. there is no other way to do the work
   B. it creates respect for authority
   C. it avoids misunderstandings
   D. they are not expected to think

17. A porter need NOT be in uniform when   17._____

    A. doing dirty work
    B. on his day off
    C. reporting *off* duty
    D. relieving the railroad clerk

Questions 18-25.

DIRECTIONS: Questions 18 through 25 are to be answered on the basis of the information
contained in the safety rules given below. Read these rules carefully before
answering these questions.

TRACKMEN SAFETY RULES ON EMERGENCY ALARM SYSTEM

In case of an emergency requiring the removal of high voltage power from the contact
rail, any trackman seeing such emergency shall immediately operate the nearest emergency
alarm box, and then immediately use the emergency telephone alongside the box to notify
the trainmaster of the nature of the trouble. High voltage will be turned on again only by telephone order from an employee specifically having such authority. The location of this equipment along the trackway is indicated by a blue light. Trackmen are required to know the
location of such boxes and the procedure to follow in order to have high voltage contact rail
power removed on sections of elevated structure trackway which may not be equipped with
emergency alarm boxes.

18. The location of an emergency alarm box is indicated by a(n) _____ light.   18._____

    A. red   B. orange   C. green   D. blue

19. Operating an emergency alarm box   19._____

    A. calls the fire department
    B. removes power
    C. lights a blue light
    D. restores power

20. All trackmen   20._____

    A. have the authority to have power restored
    B. should know the location of emergency alarm boxes
    C. must call the trainmaster before operating an emergency alarm box
    D. do not have the right to operate an emergency alarm box

21. On a track having trains in operation, a nearby emergency alarm box would PROBABLY   21._____
be operated if

    A. an employee cuts his hand
    B. the emergency telephone rings
    C. the blue light goes on
    D. a break is found in a running track rail

22. After operating an emergency alarm box, the trackman should use the emergency telephone immediately to speak to   22.____

    A. his supervisor   B. the trainmaster
    C. the station agent   D. his co-workers

23. It would be MOST important to have power restored as quickly as possible in order to reduce   23.____

    A. power waste   B. train damage
    C. train delays   D. fire hazard

24. If there are no emergency alarm boxes along a trackway, trackmen   24.____

    A. cannot have power shut off
    B. are not required to act in an emergency
    C. can have power shut off by following the proper procedure
    D. are forbidden to use the emergency telephone

25. On elevated structure trackways,   25.____

    A. emergency alarm boxes may not be found
    B. train delays never occur
    C. the trainmaster is not notified on power removal
    D. power is never removed

KEY (CORRECT ANSWERS)

1. C		11. A
2. D		12. B
3. D		13. C
4. C		14. B
5. D		15. D
6. A		16. C
7. C		17. B
8. B		18. D
9. D		19. B
10. C		20. B

21. D
22. B
23. C
24. C
25. A

TEST 3

DIRECTIONS: Each question or incomplete statement is followed by several suggested answers or completions. Select the one that BEST answers the question or completes the statement. *PRINT THE LETTER OF THE CORRECT ANSWER IN THE SPACE AT THE RIGHT.*

Questions 1-5.

DIRECTIONS: Questions 1 through 5 are to be answered on the basis of the paragraphs shown below covering the supply duties of assistant station supervisors. Refer to these paragraphs when answering these questions.

SUPPLY DUTIES OF ASSISTANT STATION SUPERVISORS

The assistant station supervisors on the 8 A.M. to 4 P.M. tour will be responsible for the ordering of porter cleaning supplies and will inventory individual stations under their jurisdiction in order to maintain the necessary supplies to insure proper sanitary standards. They will be responsible not only for the ordering of such supplies but will see to it that ordered supplies are distributed as required in accordance with order supply sheets. Assistant station supervisors on the 4 P.M. to 12 Midnight and 12 Midnight to 8 A.M. shift will cooperate with the A.M. station supervisor to properly control supplies.

The 4 P.M. to 12 Midnight assistant station supervisors will be responsible for the ordering and control of all stationery supplies used by railroad clerks in the performance of their duties. They will also see that supplies are kept in a neat and orderly manner. The assistant station supervisors in charge of *Supply Storerooms* will see to it that material so ordered will be given to the porters for delivery to the respective booths. Cooperation of all supervision applies in this instance.

The 12 Midnight to 8 A.M. assistant station supervisors will be responsible for the storing of materials delivered by special work train (sawdust, etc.). They will also see that all revenue bags which are torn, dirty, etc. are picked up and sent to the field office for delivery to the bag room.

Any supplies needed other than those distributed on regular supply days will be requested by submitting a requisition to the supply control desk for emergency delivery.

1. The assistant station supervisors who are responsible for ordering all stationery supplies   1.____
    used by railroad clerks are the ones on the _____ tour.

    A. 8 A.M. to 4 P.M.   B. 4 P.M. to 12 Midnight
    C. 12 Midnight to 8 A.M.   D. 4 P.M. to 2 P.M.

2. Storing of materials delivered by special work trains is the responsibility of assistant sta-   2.____
    tion supervisors on the _____ tour.

    A. 8 A.M. to 4 P.M.   B. 4 P.M. to 12 Midnight
    C. 12 Midnight to 8 A.M.   D. 4 P.M. to 2 P.M.

3. Torn revenue bags should be picked up and sent FIRST to   3.____

    A. the bag room   B. the supply control desk
    C. a supply storeroom   D. the field office

4. To obtain an emergency delivery of supplies on a day other than a regular supply day, a   4.____
requisition should be submitted to the

    A. appropriate zone office   B. appropriate field office
    C. supply control desk   D. station supervisor

5. The assistant station supervisor responsible for ordering porter cleaning supplies will   5.____
inventory individual stations PRIMARILY for the end purpose of

    A. insuring proper sanitary standards
    B. maintaining necessary supplies
    C. keeping track of supplies
    D. distributing supplies fairly

Questions 6-10.

DIRECTIONS: Questions 6 through 10 are to be answered on the basis of the paragraphs
                shown below entitled POSTING OF DIVERSION OF SERVICE NOTICES.
                Refer to these paragraphs when answering these questions.

POSTING OF DIVERSION OF SERVICE NOTICES

The following procedures concerning the receiving and posting of service diversion
notices will be strictly adhered to:

Assistant station supervisors who receive notices will sign a receipt and return it to the
Station Department Office. It will be their responsibility to ensure that all notices are posted at
affected stations and a notation made in the transmittal logs. All excess notices will be tied
and a notation made thereon, indicating the stations and the date notices were posted, and
the name and pass number of the assistant station supervisor posting same. The word
EXCESS is to be boldly written on bundled notices and the bundle placed in a conspicuous
location. When loose notices, without any notations, are discovered in any field office, assistant station supervisor's office, or other Station Department locations, the matter is to be thoroughly investigated to make sure proper distribution has been completed. All stations where
a diversion of service exists must be contacted daily by the assistant station supervisor covering that group and hour to ensure that a sufficient number of notices are posted and employees are aware of the situation. In any of the above circumstances, notation is to be made in
the supervisory log. Station supervisors will be responsible for making certain all affected stations in their respective groups have notices posted and for making spot checks each day
diversions are in effect.

6. An assistant station supervisor who has signed a receipt upon receiving service diver-   6.____
sion notices must return the

    A. notice to the Station Department office
    B. receipt to the Station Department office
    C. receipt and the transmittal log to the affected stations
    D. transmittal log after making a notation in it

7. Of the following, the information which is NOT required to be written on a bundle of
   excess notices is the   7._____

    A. names of the stations where the notices were posted
    B. time of day when the notices were posted
    C. date when the notices were posted
    D. name and pass number of the assistant station supervisor posting the notices

8. If loose notices without notations on them are found, the situation should be investigated
   to make sure that the   8._____

    A. notices are properly returned to the Station Department
    B. assistant station supervisor responsible for the error is found
    C. notices are correct for the diversion involved
    D. notices have been distributed properly

9. To insure that employees are aware of a diversion in service, an assistant station supervisor covering the group and hour when a diversion exists must contact the involved sta-   9._____
   tions

    A. immediately after the diversion
    B. on an hourly basis
    C. on a daily basis
    D. as often as possible

10. To make certain affected stations have notices posted when diversions occur, spot
    checks should be made by   10._____

    A. station supervisors daily
    B. station supervisors when necessary
    C. assistant station supervisors daily
    D. assistant station supervisors when necessary

Questions 11-15.

DIRECTIONS: Questions 11 through 15 are to be answered on the basis of the following
              paragraph entitled PROCEDURE FOR FLAGGING DISABLED TRAIN.

PROCEDURE FOR FLAGGING DISABLED TRAIN

    If at any time it becomes necessary to operate a train from other than the forward cab of
the leading car, a qualified Rapid Transit Transportation Department employee must be stationed on the forward end. The motorman and the aforesaid qualified employee must have a
clear understanding as to the signals to be used between them as well as to the method of
operation. They must know, by actual test, that they have communication between them.
Flagging signals should be given at short intervals while train is in motion. If train is carrying
passengers, they must be discharged at the next station. Motormen operating from other than
the forward cab of the leading car must not advance the controller beyond the *series position*.

11. The qualified employee stationed at the forward end must NOT be a   11._____

    A. motorman   B. conductor
    C. motorman instructor   D. road car inspector

12. While the train is in motion, the employees stationed at the forward end should give a   12.____
    flagging signal

    A. at frequent intervals
    B. every time the train is about to pass a fixed signal
    C. only when he wants the train speed changed
    D. only when he wants to check his understanding with the motorman

13. Motormen operating from other than the leading car must NOT advance the controller   13.____
    beyond

    A. switching   B. series   C. multiple   D. parallel

14. Considering the actual conditions on a passenger train in the subway, the MOST practi-   14.____
    cal method of communication between the motorman and the employee at the forward
    end would be by using the

    A. train public address system   B. buzzer signals
    C. whistle signals   D. lantern signals

15. The BEST reason for discharging passengers at the next station under these conditions   15.____
    is that

    A. carrying passengers would cause additional delays
    B. it is not possible to operate safely
    C. the motorman cannot see the station stop markers
    D. the four lights at the front of the train will be red

Questions 16-25.

DIRECTIONS: Questions 16 through 25, inclusive, are based on the description given in the
               following special assignment for a group of cleaners. Read the description care-
               fully before answering these questions. Be sure to consider ONLY the informa-
               tion contained in these paragraphs.

SPECIAL ASSIGNMENT

A special assignment of washing the ceilings and the tile walls of a number of stations on
a particular line was given to a group of railroad cleaners. The stations included in the assignment were both local and express stations, and the only means of transferring between the
uptown and the downtown trains without going to the street was to be found at the express
stations. The stations to be cleaned were 2nd Street, 9th Street, 16th Street, 22nd Street,
29th Street, 36th Street, 44th Street, 52nd Street, 60th Street, and 69th Street. Of these, the
express stations were located at 16th Street, 44th Street, and 69th Street.

Only the uptown sides of the stations were to be cleaned, as another gang was to clean
the downtown sides. The cleaning operations were to start at 2nd Street and progress
uptown. The materials furnished to perform this work consisted of pails, soap, long-handled
brushes, mops, rags, and canvas covers for scales and vending machines.

The instructions were to scrub a surface first with a brush that had been immersed in a
pail of soapy water, and then follow up by brushing with clear water. Any equipment on stations that was left uncovered and was splashed in the cleaning process was to be wiped
clean with a rag.

16. The total number of different kinds of materials furnished to do the work of the special assignment was   16.____

     A. 5   B. 6   C. 7   D. 8

17. Benches on station platforms were to be   17.____

     A. moved out of the work area   B. covered with canvas
     C. wiped clean with a rag if splashed   D. rinsed with clear water

18. Of the materials furnished, the instructions did NOT definitely call for the use of   18.____

     A. mops   B. brushes   C. pails   D. rags

19. The FIRST operation cleaners were instructed to do was to   19.____

     A. clean walls with scouring cleanser
     B. scrub ceilings with clear water
     C. wipe vending machines clean with rags
     D. scrub surfaces with soapy water

20. Furnished materials that were NOT used in the washing of ceilings included   20.____

     A. soap   B. pails   C. rags   D. water

21. Long-handled brushes were probably furnished because   21.____

     A. ladders cannot be used on stations
     B. such brushes are easier to handle than ordinary brushes
     C. a better job can be done, since both hands are used
     D. some areas could not be reached otherwise

22. Of the total number of stations included in the assignment, the number which were express stations was   22.____

     A. 3   B. 7   C. 10   D. 20

23. A cleaner working in the *uptown* gang at 52nd Street Station was sent by his supervisor to get some supplies from the *downtown* gang which happened to be working at the same station.
The cleaner would have displayed good judgment if he   23.____

     A. boarded a downtown train to 44th Street, crossed over, and then boarded an uptown train
     B. descended to the tracks and crossed over cautiously
     C. boarded an uptown train to 69th Street, crossed over, and then boarded a down-town train
     D. went directly up to the street and crossed over

24. After finishing the assigned work at 44th Street, the men on this assignment were sched-   24.___
uled to go next to _____ Street.

    A. 16th   B. 36th   C. 52nd   D. 69th

25. A passenger at 29th Street wishing to transfer from a downtown local to an uptown local   25.___
without paying an additional fare should transfer at _____ Street.

    A. 44th   B. 16th   C. 36th   D. 22nd

KEY (CORRECT ANSWERS)

1.	B		11.	D
2.	C		12.	A
3.	D		13.	B
4.	C		14.	B
5.	A		15.	A
6.	B		16.	B
7.	B		17.	C
8.	D		18.	A
9.	C		19.	D
10.	A		20.	C

21.	D
22.	A
23.	D
24.	C
25.	B

ARITHMETICAL REASONING
EXAMINATION SECTION
TEST 1

DIRECTIONS: Each question or incomplete statement is followed by several suggested answers or completions. Select the one that BEST answers the question or completes the statement. *PRINT THE LETTER OF THE CORRECT ANSWER IN THE SPACE AT THE RIGHT.*

1. The sum of the fractions 3/32, 3/16, 3/8, and 3/4 is equal to   1._____

    A. 1 13/32   B. 1 5/16   C. 1 7/8   D. 3

2. If a maintainer earns $11.52 per hour, and time and one-half for overtime, his gross sal-   2._____
ary for a week in which he works 5 hours over his regular 40 hours should be

    A. $460.80   B. $518.80   C. $547.20   D. $578.80

3. If the diameter of a shaft must be 2.620 inches plus or minus .002 inches, the shaft will   3._____
be SATISFACTORY if it has a diameter of _____ inches.

    A. 2.518   B. 2.600   C. 2.617   D. 2.621

4. A bus part costs $275 per 100 when purchased from a vendor. The bus part could be   4._____
made in the bus machine shop at a labor cost of $60 for 50 units, with material and other
costs amounting to $25 for 25 units.
If 100 such parts were made in the bus shop, there would be a saving of

    A. $55   B. $95   C. $140   D. $165

5. The sum of 9/16", 11/32", 15/64", and 1 3/32" is MOST NEARLY   5._____

    A. 2.234"   B. 2.134"   C. 2.334"   D. 2.214"

6. The diameter of a circle whose circumference is 14.5" is MOST NEARLY   6._____

    A. 4.62"   B. 4.81"   C. 4.72"   D. 4.51"

7. A bus part cost $90 per 100 when purchased from a vendor. The bus part could be made   7._____
in the bus machine shop at a labor cost of $20 for 50 units and material and other costs
amounting to $10 for 25 units.
If 100 such parts are made in the bus shop, there would be a saving of

    A. $10   B. $30   C. $40   D. $60

8. A bus storage battery having a 300 ampere-hour capacity is 50% discharged.   8._____
If the bus running schedule for the day is such that the battery will be charging at an
average rate of 30 amperes for 2 1/2 hours and discharging at an average rate of 9
amperes for 5 hours, then at the end of the day, the battery will be APPROXIMATELY

    A. at full charge   B. 75% charged
    C. 60% charged   D. 50% charged

9. If the total time allowance for replacing the glass in a broken bus window is 75 minutes, how many jobs of this kind would a maintainer be expected to do in 40 hours of work?   9._____

   A.   32   B.   40   C.   60   D.   72

10. A certain rod is tapered so that it changes diameter at a rate of 1/4 inch per foot of length. If the tapered rod is 3 inches long, then the difference in diameter between the two ends is MOST NEARLY   10._____

   A.   0.250"   B.   0.187"   C.   0.135"   D.   0.062"

11. How many 9 1/2 inch long pieces of copper tubing can be cut from a 20-foot length of tubing?   11._____

   A.   24   B.   25   C.   26   D.   27

12. Two splice plates must be cut from a piece of sheet steel that has an overall length of 14 3/8 inches. The plates are to be 7 5/8 inches and 5 1/4 inches long.
   If 1/16 inch is allowed for each saw cut, then how much material would be left?   12._____

   A.   1 3/8"   B.   1 1/2"   C.   1 5/8"   D.   1 3/4"

13. A maintainer requires several lengths of tubing for oil lines as follows: 12 7/16 inches, 14 5/16 inches, 9 3/16 inches, 9 1/8 inches, 6 1/4 inches, and 5 inches.
   The TOTAL length of tubing required is MOST NEARLY _____, feet.   13._____

   A.   2   B.   3   C.   4   D.   5

14. Two-thirds of 10 feet is MOST NEARLY   14._____

   A.   6'2"   B.   6'8"   C.   6'11"   D.   7'1"

15. You are directed to pick up a tray load of brake shoes. The combined weight of tray and brake shoes is 4,000 pounds. Assume that each brake shoe weighs 40 pounds and the tray weighs 240 pounds.
   The number of brake shoes in the tray is MOST NEARLY   15._____

   A.   88   B.   94   C.   100   D.   106

16. A maintainer earns $12.44 per hour, and time and one-half for overtime over 40 hours. Each week, 15 percent of his total salary is deducted for social security and taxes. Also, each week a $18.00 deduction is made for a savings bond and a $9.00 deduction is made for a charitable organization.
   If he works a total of 46 hours in a week, his take-home pay for that week is   16._____

   A. $609.56   B. $518.10   C. $491.12   D. $410.70

17. A rectangularly-shaped repair facility for light trucks is 160 feet wide and 260 feet long. A 10-foot space is provided along each wall for benches and equipment. A 60-foot wide area in the middle of the floor is to remain clear for its entire 260 foot length. The entrance to the shop is at one end of this open area.
   Assuming that there are no columns to contend with, the MAXIMUM area available for parking of trucks is _____ sq. ft.   17._____

   A.   15,600   B.   19,200   C.   26,000   D.   41,600

18. A criterion is established that limits the yearly major repair expenses to 30% of the current value of the equipment. Equipment is depreciated at a rate of 20% of its original cost each year. A truck purchased on January 1, 2000 for $9,000 had a reconditioned engine installed in February 2003 at a total cost of $900.
The amount of money available for additional major repairs on this truck in 2003 is

    A. none   B. $180   C. $360   D. $720

18.____

19. Twenty carburetors are ordered for your shop by the Purchasing Department. The terms are list, less 30% less 10%, less 5%.
If the list price of a carburetor is $70 and all terms are met upon delivery, the charges to your budget will be

    A. $1,359.60   B. $1,085.40   C. $837.90   D. $630.80

19.____

20. The sum of the fractions 7/16", 11/16", 5/32", and 7/8" is MOST NEARLY

    A. 2.1753"   B. 2.1563"   C. 1.9522"   D. 1.9463"

20.____

21. If 750 feet of wire weighs 60 lbs., the number of pounds that 150 feet will weigh is MOST NEARLY

    A. 12   B. 10   C. 8   D. 6

21.____

22. A steel rod 19.750" long is to have three pieces cut from its length. One piece is to be 3.250" long, the second 6.500" long, and the third piece 5.375".
If .125" is allowed for each cut, the length of the material left over is

    A. 3.750"   B. 4.250"   C. 4.500"   D. 5.150"

22.____

23. If the distance between the north and south terminals is 10.8 miles and a train makes six roundtrips, then the total travel mileage would be NEAREST _____ miles.

    A. 22   B. 65   C. 130   D. 145

23.____

24. If the thickness of material worn from a car wheel is approximately 1/16 inch off the diameter in 20,000 miles of travel, the wheel diameter will be reduced from 33 inches to 32 3/4 inches after _____ miles.

    A. 60,000   B. 80,000   C. 100,000   D. 120,000

24.____

25. If the distance between the north and south terminals is 11.3 miles and a train makes five roundtrips, then the total travel mileage would be NEAREST _____ miles.

    A. 23   B. 55   C. 115   D. 130

25.____

KEY (CORRECT ANSWERS)

1.	A		11.	B
2.	C		12.	A
3.	D		13.	D
4.	A		14.	B
5.	A		15.	B
6.	A		16.	C
7.	A		17.	B
8.	C		18.	B
9.	A		19.	C
10.	D		20.	B

21.	A
22.	B
23.	C
24.	B
25.	C

SOLUTIONS TO PROBLEMS

1. $\dfrac{3}{32}+\dfrac{3}{16}+\dfrac{3}{8}+\dfrac{3}{4}=\dfrac{45}{32}=1\dfrac{13}{32}$

2. Gross salary = ($11.52)(40) + ($17.28)(5) = $547.20

3. 2.620 ± .002 means from 2.618 to 2.622. The only selection in this range is 2.621.

4. ($60)($\dfrac{100}{50}$)+($25)($\dfrac{100}{25}$) $220 if made in the bus shop. Savings = $275 - $220 = $55

5. 9/16" + 11/32" + 15/64" + 1 3/32" =143/64 = 2 15/64" ≈ 2.234"

6. Diameter = 14.5" ÷ π ≈ 4.62"

7. ($20)($\dfrac{100}{50}$)+($10)($\dfrac{100}{25}$) = $80 if made in the bus shop. Savings = $90 - $80 = $10

8. [150 + [(30)(2 1/2)] - [(9)(5)] = [150+75] - 45 = 180, and 180/300 = 60%

9. (40)(60) ÷ 75 = 32

10. (1/4")(3/12) = 1/16" ≈ .062"

11. (20)(12) = 240", and 240" ÷ 9 1/2" ≈ 25.3, rounded down to 25 pieces of tubing

12. 14 3/8" - 7 5/8" - 5 1/4" - 1/16" = 1 3/8"

13. 12 7/16" + 14 5/16" + 9 3/16" + 9 1/8" + 6 1/4" + 5" = 56 5/16" ≈ 5 ft.

14. (2/3)(10') = 6 2/3' = 6'8"

15. 4000 - 240 = 3760 lbs. Then, 3760 ÷ 40 = 94 brake shoes

16. Take-home pay = ($12.44)(40)+($18.66)(6) - .15[($12.44)(40) + ($18.66)(6)] - $18.00 - $9.00 = $491.126 ≈ $491.12

17. Subtracting the area for benches and equipment would leave an area of 240' by 140'. Now, deduct the 60' width. Final area = (240')(80') = 19,200 sq.ft.

18. In 2003, the value of the truck = $9000 - (3)(.20)($9000) = $3600 The limit of the expenses for repairs = (.30)($3600) = $1080 After installing engine, $1080 - $900 = $180 left for additional major repairs.

19. (20)($70)(.70)(.90)(.95) = $837.90

20. 7/16" + 11/16" + 5/32" + 7/8" = 69/32" ≈ 2.1563"

21. (150/750)(60) = 12 lbs.

22. 19.750" - 3.250" - 6.500" - 5.375" - .125" - .125" - .125" = 4.250" left over

23. (6)(10.8)(2) = 129.6 ≈ 130 miles

24. 33" - 32 3/4" = 1/4". Then, (1/4 ÷ 1/16)(20,000) = 80,000 miles

25. (5)(11.3)(2) = 113 miles, closest to 115 miles

TEST 2

DIRECTIONS: Each question or incomplete statement is followed by several suggested answers or completions. Select the one that BEST answers the question or completes the statement. *PRINT THE LETTER OF THE CORRECT ANSWER IN THE SPACE AT THE RIGHT.*

1. In looking over an alteration job on car bodies, you find that 96 pieces of 1" x 1" x 1'6" long square steel stock are needed to do this job. Steel weighs 480 lbs. per cu. ft. and costs $0.12 per lb.
   The total cost of this material is MOST NEARLY

   A. $40.00   B. $60.00   C. $80.00   D. $100.00   1.____

2. Assume that the breakdown cost of a particular motor job is as follows: 2.____
   Parts $160.00
   Labor   75.00
   Overhead   30.00
   The percentage of the total cost for labor is MOST NEARLY

   A. 20%   B. 25%   C. 28%   D. 32%

3. The engine hydraulic system and transmission on a certain type of tractor use the same   3.____
   type oil. This oil is delivered in 55 gallon drums.
   How many drums are needed to make all three changes on 10 of these tractors
   whose- capacities are the following:
   Engine   58 quarts
   Transmission   70 quarts
   Hydraulic system   22 gallons
   _____ drums.

   A. 100   B. 50   C. 54   D. 10

4. A new shop layout requires the following: 4.____
   1,000   sq. ft. for tool room
   3,000   sq. ft. for parts room
   10,000 sq. ft. for service bays
   5,500   sq. ft. for isles
   The building should be AT LEAST _____ yards wide and 70 yards long.

   A. 10   B. 20   C. 25   D. 30

5. When filling a diesel engine cooling system, the mix required is 80% antifreeze and 20%   5.____
   water. You are required to fill seven systems containing 30 gals. each. The number of 5
   gallon cans of antifreeze that are required is MOST NEARLY

   A. 210   B. 168   C. 34   D. 26

6. The floors of 2 cars are to be painted with a special test paint. Assume that the floor area   6.____
   in each car is 600 square feet. A gallon of this paint will cover 400 square feet.
   The number of gallons of this paint that you should pick up at the storeroom to paint
   the two car floors would be

   A. 6   B. 5   C. 4   D. 3

7. Assume that you are sent to the storeroom for 1,000 of 600-volt contact tips which are to be distributed equally to 5 foremen, but you find that the storeroom can only supply you with 825.
If you distribute these 825 tips equally to the 5 foremen, the number of tips that each foreman will receive is

    A.   165   B.   175   C.   190   D.   200

7.____

8. You are asked to fill six 5-gallon cans of oil from a full drum containing 52 gallons.
When you have filled the six cans, the number of gallons of oil left in the drum will be MOST NEARLY

    A.   14   B.   16   C.   22   D.   30

8.____

9. A certain wire rope is made up of 6 strands, each strand containing 19 wires.
The TOTAL number of wires in this wire rope is

    A.   25   B.   96   C.   114   D.   144

9.____

10. The hook should be the weakest part of any crane, hoist, or sling.
According to this statement, if a particular hook has a rated capacity of 2 1/2 tons, then the MAXIMUM load that should be lifted with this hook is _____ pounds.

    A.   150   B.   3,000   C.   5,000   D.   5,500

10.____

11. Assume that 2 car wheels weigh 635 pounds each and are attached to an axle weighing 1,260 pounds.
The total weight of this assembly is MOST NEARLY _____ pounds.

    A.   1,270   B.   1,520   C.   1,895   D.   2,530

11.____

12. If an employee authorizes his employer to deduct 4% of his $300 weekly salary for a savings bond, the MINIMUM number of weekly deductions required to get enough money to buy a bond costing $36 is

    A.   3   B.   6   C.   8   D.   9

12.____

13. In weighing out a truckful of scrap metal, the scale reads 21,496 lbs.
If the empty truck weighs 9,879 lbs., the amount of scrap metal, in pounds, is MOST NEARLY

    A.   10,507   B.   10,602   C.   11,617   D.   12,617

13.____

14. Four trays of material are placed on the body of a delivery truck for delivery to the inspection shop. Each tray is 4 feet wide and 4 feet long.
If these trays are placed side by side on the floor of the delivery truck, together they will cover an area of the floor MOST NEARLY _____ square feet.

    A.   32   B.   48   C.   64   D.   72

14.____

15. Assume that you are operating a degreasing tank and its tray holds 5 gear cases. It takes 40 minutes to clean one tray of gear cases.
At the end of 6 hours of operation (excluding lunch break and loading and unloading time), the number of gear cases cleaned will be

    A.   30   B.   36   C.   45   D.   50

15.____

16. If a serviceman's weekly gross salary is $160 and 20% is deducted for taxes, his take-home pay is   16.____

    A. $120   B. $128   C. $140   D. $144

Questions 17-18.

DIRECTIONS: Questions 17 and 18 are to be answered on the basis of the following paragraph.

The car maintenance department is considering the purchase of a certain car part from Manufacturer X for $140. An equivalent part can be purchased from Manufacturer Y for $100. The part made by Manufacturer X must be reconditioned every 3 years, using material costing $30 and requiring 6 hours of labor. The part made by Manufacturer Y must be reconditioned every 1 1/2 years, using material costing $24 and requiring 5 hours of labor. The maintainer's rate of pay is $12 per hour.

17. The cost of operating with the part made by Manufacturer X (excluding the first cost) is MOST NEARLY _____ per year.   17.____

    A. $30   B. $32   C. $34   D. $42

18. The total cost of operating with the part made by Manufacturer Y over a period of 12 years, including the first cost of the part and assuming the part is scrapped at the end of 12 years, is MOST NEARLY   18.____

    A. $472   B. $572   C. $688   D. $772

19. The area of the steel plate shown in the sketch at the right is _____ sq. ft.   19.____

    A. 16
    B. 18
    C. 20
    D. 22

(Sketch labels: 4 FT, 1 FT, 2 FT, 4 FT, 7 FT)

20. A car part made by a Manufacturer X has a purchase cost of $7,500 and a life of 5 years. It requires a yearly maintenance cost of $50. Manufacturer Y offers a similar part of this type for $4,800, with a life of 3 years and a yearly maintenance cost of $75.
By purchasing the part offering a better overall value, the yearly savings per unit purchased would be   20.____

    A. $115   B. $125   C. $135   D. $140

21. A car part can be overhauled at the rate of 12 parts per hour. Each part requires new material costing $6 each. If the labor cost is $14 per hour, one part can be overhauled for a total cost (labor plus material) of MOST NEARLY   21.____

    A. $6.64   B. $7.16   C. $7.46   D. $8.20

22. A car part costs $150 per 50 units when purchased in a finished condition from a vendor. The car part can be made in the shop at a total cost of $2.20 per unit, when made on a machine which can be purchased for $1,000. The MINIMUM number of parts which must be made on this machine before the savings equal the cost of the machine is

    A.   850   B.   1,000   C.   1,250   D.   1,500

22.____

23. A pound of a certain type of metal washer contains 360 washers.
If 1/4 of the material of each washer is removed by enlarging the center of each washer, the number of washers to the pound should then be MOST NEARLY

    A.   280   B.   300   C.   380   D.   480

23.____

24. A maintainer earns $10.84 per hour, and time and one-half for overtime. Ten percent of his total salary earned is deducted from his paycheck for social security and taxes. He also contributes $5.00 per week to a charitable organization. No other deductions are made.
If he works 2 hours over his basic 40 hours, his weekly take-home pay should be MOST NEARLY

    A. $466.12   B. $419.50   C. $414.50   D. $410.60

24.____

25. A car part costs $130 per 100 units if purchased from a vendor. The car part can be made on a machine which can be purchased for $1,000. Assume that this machine has a production life of 20,000 units with no salvage value, and that all shop costs amount to $80 per 100 units turned out in the shop.
The money that would be SAVED during the life of the machine would be

    A. $800   B. $8,000   C. $9,000   D. $18,000

25.____

KEY (CORRECT ANSWERS)

1.	B		11.	D
2.	C		12.	A
3.	D		13.	C
4.	D		14.	C
5.	C		15.	C
6.	D		16.	B
7.	A		17.	C
8.	C		18.	C
9.	C		19.	C
10.	C		20.	B

21.	B
22.	C
23.	D
24.	C
25.	C

SOLUTIONS TO PROBLEMS

1. Total cost ≈ (96)(.01)(480)(.12) ≈ $55, which is closest to $60. Note that 1" x 1" x 1'6" ≈ (1/12')(1/12')(3/2')= 1/96 ≈ .01 cu. ft.

2. Labor = $75 ÷ $265 ≈ 28%

3. (10)(14.5+17.5+22) = 540. Then, 540 ÷ 55 ≈ 10 drums

4. Total sq.ft. = 19,500, which is 2166 2/3 sq.yds.

    Then, 2166 2/3 ÷ 70 ≈ 30.95 or 31

5. Amount of antifreeze = (.80)(7)(.30) = 168 gallons.

    Then, 2166 2/3 ÷ 70 ≈ 30.95 or 31

6. (600+600) ÷ 400 = 3 gallons

7. 825 ÷ 5 = 165 for each foreman

8. 52 - (6)(5) = 22 gallons left

9. (19)(6) = 114 wires

10. (2 1/2)(2000) = 5000 pounds

11. (2)(635) + 1260 = 2530 pounds

12. ($300)(.04) = $12. Then, $36 ÷ $12 = 3 weekly deductions

13. 21,496 - 9,879 = 11,617 pounds

14. 4(4')(4') = 64 sq.ft.

15. 6 hrs ÷ 2/3 hr. = 9 trays = 45 gear cases cleaned

16. Take-home pay = ($160)(.80) = $128

17. ($30) + (6)($12) = $102 for 3 yrs = $34 per year

18. 100 + 7(24) + 7(60) = 688

19. Separate the figure into regions as follows:

    I: 1'x2' = 2 sq.ft.

    II: 3'x4' = 12 sq.ft.

    III: (3'x4') ÷ 2' =6 sq.ft.

    Total = 20 sq.ft.

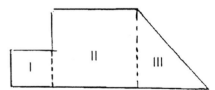

20. Manufacturer X: $7500 + ($50)(5) = $7750, so the cost per year is $7750 ÷ 5 = $1550.
    Manufacturer Y: $4800 + (3)($75) = $5025, so the cost per year is $5025 ÷ 3 = $1675
    Using Manufacturer X, savings = $125 per year

21. Cost of 12 parts = (12)($6) + $14 = $86. Then, cost of one part = $86 ÷ 12 ≈ $7.16

22. Savings per unit is &150/50 - $2.20 = $.80. Then, $1000 ÷ $.80 = 1250

23. 1 - 1/4 - 3/4. Then, 360 ÷ 3/4 = 480

24. Take-home pay = [($10.84)(40)+($16.26)(2)][.90] - $5 ≈ $414.50

25. Amount if purchased from a vendor = $130(200) = $26,000

    Using the machine, amount = $1000 + ($80)(200) = $17,000. Amount saved = $9000

TEST 3

DIRECTIONS: Each question or incomplete statement is followed by several suggested answers or completions. Select the one that BEST answers the question or completes the statement. *PRINT THE LETTER OF THE CORRECT ANSWER IN THE SPACE AT THE RIGHT.*

1. A Cat 983 Traxcavator can make a complete loading cycle from bank to truck and back to bank in 25 seconds.
   If the bucket contains 4 cu. yds. of loose material, the MINIMUM amount of material that an operator should load in 4 hours is _____ cubic yards.

   A.   2,304   B.   2,100   C.   1,896   D.   576   1.____

2. An excavation is 12' x 18' x 15' and is to be dug by a Cat 983 Traxcavator with 3 cubic yards of solid material excavated per pass.
   The MINIMUM number of passes required to dig the hole is _____ passes.

   A.   40   B.   46   C.   120   D.   126   2.____

3. A Cat D8 tractor and 463 scraper can haul 22 cubic yards of cover material per trip.
   If it is required to cover an area 1,000 feet by 100 feet to a depth of 2 feet, the MINI-MUM number of trips that will be required is MOST NEARLY

   A.   284   B.   337   C.   385   D.   421   3.____

4. Gravel weighs 2,800 pounds per cubic yard.
   In order to carry 42,000 pounds of gravel, the capacity of a truck must be AT LEAST _____ cubic yards.

   A.   10   B.   12   C.   15   D.   18   4.____

5. The average capacity of an Athey Wagon is 60 cubic yards. The Cat D8 tractor pulls 2 wagons.
   The MINIMUM number of trips to the fill that would be required to empty a barge loaded with 1,000 cubic yards of refuse is

   A.   9   B.   17   C.   30   D.   90   5.____

6. When pulling 2 Athey trailers, the operator of a Cat D8 tractor can make a roundtrip from the crane to the fill and back in 15 minutes.
   Assuming that delays and breaks allow the man to work productively for 75% of the shift, the MAXIMUM number of trips that the operator can make in an 8-hour shift is

   A.   43   B.   32   C.   24   D.   16   6.____

7. In plowing a street which is 24 feet wide, a motor grader can make an 8-ft. wide pass, with a 2-ft. overlap.
   If a roundtrip takes 4 minutes, the MINIMUM time needed to plow this street should be _____ minutes.

   A.   12   B.   16   C.   24   D.   32   7.____

8. A scraper is loaded with 23 cubic yards of sand weighing 100 pounds per cubic foot.
   The weight of the load, in tons, is MOST NEARLY

   A.   20   B.   30   C.   40   D.   60   8.____

9. Assume a crankcase oil change of 6 quarts for every 150 service hours. How many 42 gallon drums of oil are required for 8,400 total service hours?

    A. 5   B. 2   C. 1   D. 1 1/3

9._____

10. Assume that a ruler is marked in 10ths of a foot instead of in inches. 5 tenths on this ruler would be

    A. 4"   B. 5"   C. 6"   D. 7"

10._____

11. A truck load of 1 1/2" stone from a 10 cubic yard truck will spread an area APPROXI-MATELY _____ long, 6" deep, and _____ wide.

    A. 50'; 10'   B. 10'; 5'   C. 54'; 10'   D. 45'; 5'

11._____

12. A dump truck with a body 10 ft. long, 5 ft. wide, and 4 ft. deep has a volume of _____ cubic feet.

    A. 150   B. 200   C. 250   D. 300

12._____

13. A tractor is operated on a given landfill operation during the following time intervals in one day: from 8:15 A.M. to 11:45 A.M.; from 12:30 P.M. to 6:00 P.M.; from 6:45 P.M. to 11:30 P.M.
The total net operating time, expressed in hours and minutes, is MOST NEARLY _____ hours, _____ minutes.

    A. 13; 30   B. 13; 15   C. 13; 45   D. 12; 45

13._____

14. The area of ground contact (with standard track shoes) of a late model D8 Caterpillar Tractor is 4,296 sq. in. Expressed in square feet, this is MOST NEARLY

    A. 358   B. 29.8   C. 159.3   D. 21.37

14._____

15. A towing winch develops a bare drum line pull of 11.8 tons. This force represents, in pounds,

    A. 23,850   B. 28,300   C. 23,800   D. 23,600

15._____

16. The fuel tank gauge reads about 3/4 of a full tank. If the tank capacity is 72.5 gallons, the amount of fuel in the tank is MOST NEARLY

    A. 53.2   B. 53.8   C. 54.5   D. 55.0

16._____

17. If a dump truck capable of carrying 40 2/3 cubic yards is 3/4 loaded, it is carrying, in cubic yards,

    A. 28   B. 36 1/2   C. 30 1/2   D. 28 2/3

17._____

18. A load of sand filling a truck body 6 feet long, 5 feet wide, and 3 feet deep would contain _____ cubic feet.

    A. 14   B. 90   C. 33   D. 21

18._____

Questions 19-21.

DIRECTIONS: Questions 19 through 21 are to be answered on the basis of the diagrams of balanced levers shown below. P is the center of rotation, W is the weight on the lever, and F is the balancing force.

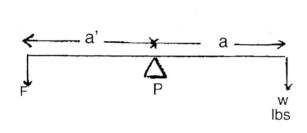 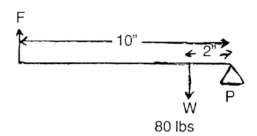

19. In Diagram 1, the force F required to balance the weight W lbs. on the lever shown is equal to _____ lbs.   19._____

    A. a/W   B. W/a   C. W   D. Wa

20. In Diagram 2, the force F required to balance the weight of 80 lbs. on the lever shown is _____ lbs.   20._____

    A. 4   B. 3   C. 16   D. 32

21. The mechanical advantage of the lever shown in Diagram 2 is   21._____

    A. 4   B. 5   C. 8   D. 12

22. The specific gravity of a liquid may be defined as the ratio of the weight of a given volume of the liquid to the weight of an equal volume of water. An empty bottle weighs 5 oz. When the bottle is filled with water, the total weight is 50 oz. When the bottle is filled with another liquid, the total weight is 95 oz.
    The specific gravity of the second liquid is MOST NEARLY   22._____

    A. .50   B. .58   C. 1.7   D. 2.0

23. If one inch is approximately equal to 2.54 centimeters, the number of inches in one meter is MOST NEARLY   23._____

    A. 14.2   B. 25.4   C. 39.4   D. 91.4

24. One-quarter divided by five-eighths is   24._____

    A. 5/32   B. 1/10   C. 2/5   D. 5/2

25. A man works on a certain job continuously, with no time off for lunch.   25._____
    If he works from 9:45 A.M. until 1:35 P.M. to finish the job, the total time which he spent on the job is MOST NEARLY _____ hours, _____ minutes.

    A. 3; 10   B. 3; 35   C. 3; 50   D. 4; 15

KEY (CORRECT ANSWERS)

1.	A		11.	C
2.	A		12.	B
3.	B		13.	C
4.	C		14.	B
5.	A		15.	D
6.	C		16.	C
7.	B		17.	C
8.	B		18.	B
9.	B		19.	C
10.	C		20.	C

21.	B
22.	D
23.	C
24.	C
25.	C

SOLUTIONS TO PROBLEMS

1. 4 hrs = (4)(60)(60) = 14,400 sec. Then, 14,400 ÷ 25 = 576 Thus, (576)(4 cu.yds.) = 2304 cu.yds.

2. (12')(18')(15') = 3240 cu.ft. = 120 cu.yds. Then, 120 ÷ 3 = 40

3. (1000')(100')(2') = 200,000 cu.ft. ≈ 7407.4 cu.yds.
   Finally, 7407.4 ÷ 22 = 336.7, rounded up to 337 trips.

4. 42,000 ÷ 2800 = 15 cu.yds.

5. (2)(60 cu.yds.) = 120 yds. Then, 1000 ÷ 120 = 8 1/3, which must be rounded up to 9 trips

6. 8 hrs ÷ 15 min = 32. Then, (32)(.75) = 24 trips

7. 24' ÷ 8' = 3; however, with a 2 ft. overlap, only 6' gets plowed. So, (24 ÷ 6)(4 min) = 16 min.

8. 23 cu.yds. = 621 cu.ft. Then, (621)(100) = 62,100 lbs.
   Finally, 62,100 ÷ 2000 ≈ 30 tons

9. 8400 ÷ 150 = 56. Then, (56)(6 qts) = 336 qts = 84 gallons
   Finally, 84 ÷ 42 = 2 drums

10. 5 tenths = (5/10)(12") = 6"

11. (54')(1/2')(10') = 270 cu.ft. = 10 cu.yds.

12. Volume = (10')(5')(4') = 200 cu.ft.

13. 3 hrs. 30 min. + 5 hrs. 30 min. + 4 hrs. 45 min. = 12 hrs. 105 min. = 13 hrs. 45 min.

14. 4296 sq.in. = 4296 ÷ 144 ≈ 29.8 sq.ft.

15. 11.8 tons = (11.8)(2000) = 23,600 lbs.

16. (72.5)(.75) = 54.375, closest to 54.5 gallons

17. (40 2/3)(3/4) = 30 1/2 cu.yds.

18. (6')(5')(3') = 90 cu.ft.

19. F = Wa/a = W lbs.

20. F = (80)(2) ÷ 10 = 16 lbs.

21. Mechanical advantage = 10/2 = 5

22. Specific gravity $= \dfrac{95-5}{50-5} = 2$

23. 1 meter = 100 cm. ≈ (100) ÷ (2.54) ≈ 39.4 in.

24. $1/4 \div 5/8 = \dfrac{1}{4} \cdot \dfrac{8}{5} = \dfrac{2}{5}$

25. 9:45 AM to 1:35 PM = 3 hrs. 50 min.

———

ANSWER SHEET

TEST NO. _____ PART _____ TITLE OF POSITION _____

(AS GIVEN IN EXAMINATION ANNOUNCEMENT - INCLUDE OPTION, IF ANY)

PLACE OF EXAMINATION _____ DATE _____

(CITY OR TOWN)   (STATE)

RATING

USE THE SPECIAL PENCIL.   MAKE GLOSSY BLACK MARKS.

Make only ONE mark for each answer.   Additional and stray marks may be counted as mistakes.   In making corrections, erase errors COMPLETELY.

ANSWER SHEET

TEST NO. _____ PART _____ TITLE OF POSITION _____

PLACE OF EXAMINATION _____ DATE _____

(CITY OR TOWN)   (STATE)

RATING

USE THE SPECIAL PENCIL.   MAKE GLOSSY BLACK MARKS.

	A B C D E		A B C D E		A B C D E		A B C D E		A B C D E
1	:: :: :: :: ::	26	:: :: :: :: ::	51	:: :: :: :: ::	76	:: :: :: :: ::	101	:: :: :: :: ::
2	:: :: :: :: ::	27	:: :: :: :: ::	52	:: :: :: :: ::	77	:: :: :: :: ::	102	:: :: :: :: ::
3	:: :: :: :: ::	28	:: :: :: :: ::	53	:: :: :: :: ::	78	:: :: :: :: ::	103	:: :: :: :: ::
4	:: :: :: :: ::	29	:: :: :: :: ::	54	:: :: :: :: ::	79	:: :: :: :: ::	104	:: :: :: :: ::
5	:: :: :: :: ::	30	:: :: :: :: ::	55	:: :: :: :: ::	80	:: :: :: :: ::	105	:: :: :: :: ::
6	:: :: :: :: ::	31	:: :: :: :: ::	56	:: :: :: :: ::	81	:: :: :: :: ::	106	:: :: :: :: ::
7	:: :: :: :: ::	32	:: :: :: :: ::	57	:: :: :: :: ::	82	:: :: :: :: ::	107	:: :: :: :: ::
8	:: :: :: :: ::	33	:: :: :: :: ::	58	:: :: :: :: ::	83	:: :: :: :: ::	108	:: :: :: :: ::
9	:: :: :: :: ::	34	:: :: :: :: ::	59	:: :: :: :: ::	84	:: :: :: :: ::	109	:: :: :: :: ::
10	:: :: :: :: ::	35	:: :: :: :: ::	60	:: :: :: :: ::	85	:: :: :: :: ::	110	:: :: :: :: ::

Make only ONE mark for each answer.   Additional and stray marks may be
counted as mistakes.   In making corrections, erase errors COMPLETELY.

	A B C D E		A B C D E		A B C D E		A B C D E		A B C D E
11	:: :: :: :: ::	36	:: :: :: :: ::	61	:: :: :: :: ::	86	:: :: :: :: ::	111	:: :: :: :: ::
12	:: :: :: :: ::	37	:: :: :: :: ::	62	:: :: :: :: ::	87	:: :: :: :: ::	112	:: :: :: :: ::
13	:: :: :: :: ::	38	:: :: :: :: ::	63	:: :: :: :: ::	88	:: :: :: :: ::	113	:: :: :: :: ::
14	:: :: :: :: ::	39	:: :: :: :: ::	64	:: :: :: :: ::	89	:: :: :: :: ::	114	:: :: :: :: ::
15	:: :: :: :: ::	40	:: :: :: :: ::	65	:: :: :: :: ::	90	:: :: :: :: ::	115	:: :: :: :: ::
16	:: :: :: :: ::	41	:: :: :: :: ::	66	:: :: :: :: ::	91	:: :: :: :: ::	116	:: :: :: :: ::
17	:: :: :: :: ::	42	:: :: :: :: ::	67	:: :: :: :: ::	92	:: :: :: :: ::	117	:: :: :: :: ::
18	:: :: :: :: ::	43	:: :: :: :: ::	68	:: :: :: :: ::	93	:: :: :: :: ::	118	:: :: :: :: ::
19	:: :: :: :: ::	44	:: :: :: :: ::	69	:: :: :: :: ::	94	:: :: :: :: ::	119	:: :: :: :: ::
20	:: :: :: :: ::	45	:: :: :: :: ::	70	:: :: :: :: ::	95	:: :: :: :: ::	120	:: :: :: :: ::
21	:: :: :: :: ::	46	:: :: :: :: ::	71	:: :: :: :: ::	96	:: :: :: :: ::	121	:: :: :: :: ::
22	:: :: :: :: ::	47	:: :: :: :: ::	72	:: :: :: :: ::	97	:: :: :: :: ::	122	:: :: :: :: ::
23	:: :: :: :: ::	48	:: :: :: :: ::	73	:: :: :: :: ::	98	:: :: :: :: ::	123	:: :: :: :: ::
24	:: :: :: :: ::	49	:: :: :: :: ::	74	:: :: :: :: ::	99	:: :: :: :: ::	124	:: :: :: :: ::
25	:: :: :: :: ::	50	:: :: :: :: ::	75	:: :: :: :: ::	100	:: :: :: :: ::	125	:: :: :: :: ::